JO SCHLEHOFER

JOY IN PARENTING

Parenting Skills with Pre-Schoolers through Adolescents

PAULIST PRESS
New York/Ramsey/Toronto

Library of Congress
Catalog Card Number: 78-58951

ISBN: 0-8091-2125-5

Published by Paulist Press
Editorial Office: 1865 Broadway, New York, N.Y. 10023
Business Office: 545 Island Road, Ramsey, N.J. 07446

Printed and bound in the
United States of America

ACKNOWLEDGEMENTS

Grateful appreciation is herein expressed to the publishers indicated for their kind
permission to quote from the following works:

"What Every Child Needs for Good Mental Health," adapted from WHAT EVERY CHILD
NEEDS FOR GOOD MENTAL HEALTH, Mental Health Association, Arlington, Virginia.
Excerpt from WHAT MAKES ME FEEL THIS WAY? by Eda Le Shan, Collier Books, New
York, N.Y. © 1972.
Excerpts from YOUR CHILD'S SELF ESTEEM by Dorothy Corkille Briggs, Doubleday,
New York, N.Y. © 1970.
Excerpt from THE VELVETEEN RABBIT by Margery Williams, reprinted with the per-
mission of Doubleday & Company Inc., New York, N.Y.
Excerpt "On Children" taken from THE PROPHET, by Kahlil Gibran, Alfred A. Knopf, Inc.,
New York, N.Y. © 1923, 1951. Reprinted by permission of the Publisher.
Excerpt from BETWEEN PARENT AND TEENAGER by Dr. Haim Ginott, Macmillan Co.,
New York, N.Y. © 1969. Reprinted with the permission of Dr. Alice L. Ginott.
Excerpt from Ann Landers Syndicated Column, reprinted with the permission of the Field
Newspaper Syndicate, Chicago, Illinois.

TABLE OF CONTENTS

INTRODUCTION 1

CHAPTER 1
SELF-ESTEEM, PARENT AND CHILD................................. 7

CHAPTER 2
AGES AND STAGES, INFANCY THROUGH ADOLESCENCE 31

CHAPTER 3
DISCIPLINE, MEANING AND ALTERNATIVES 61

CHAPTER 4
SIBLING RIVALRY, INTERACTIONS BETWEEN SIBLINGS 87

CHAPTER 5
FEELINGS AND EMOTIONS, BUILDING POSITIVE
        MENTAL HEALTH 111

CHAPTER 6
SEXUALITY, MORALITY AND VALUES...141

CHAPTER 7
SPIRITUALITY, DEVELOPING RELIGIOUS VALUES 165

ANNOTATED BIBLIOGRAPHY 186

FOREWORD

I have written this book for parents to help them with the sorrows and joys of everyday parenting. We all share a unique stage in our life when we parent. This stage crosses all boundaries of humanism without necessarily having to be labeled single parent, teenage parent, abusive parent, working parent, migrant parent, step-parent, foster parent, rich parent, poor parent, or handicapped parent. Hopefully these basic skills will bring confidence and joy to *all* parents.

I am grateful to all the parents I have worked with, for I have learned much from them. Appreciation goes to my colleagues who have reinforced my work. Sincere recognition goes to all the authors I have read and whose ideas have been incorporated into my thinking. I have made a sincere effort to give recognition where it is due. Heartfelt thanks go to those who took the time to type my manuscript. Lastly, but most importantly, my loving gratitude goes to my husband and three children who have made parenting a joyful experience for me.

The use of "he" throughout the book is for convenience only; both genders are implied.

Exercises throughout the book will enable you to develop parenting skills. Fill them out carefully. Your child is given to you by God for only a little while. Parent as well as you can. Help God develop his creation.

"A thing of beauty is a joy forever, its loveliness increases, it will never pass into nothingness" (Keats).

*Real joy comes not from ease or riches or
from praises of men,
but from doing something worthwile*

Wilfred T. Grenfill

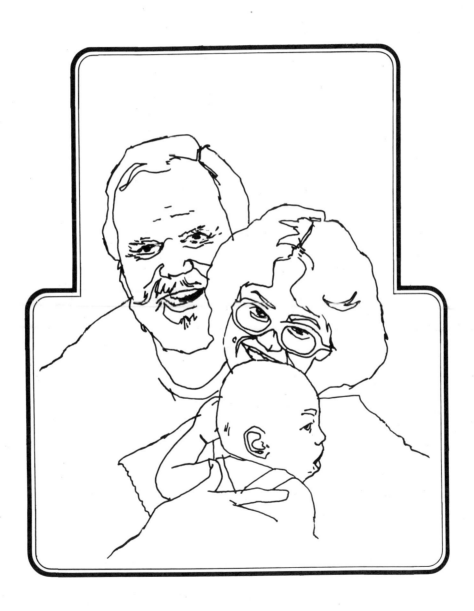

JOY IN PARENTING

"Parenthood is an endless series of small events, periodic conflicts and sudden crisis which calls for a response—love is not enough. Insight is insufficient. Good parents need skills."

Dr. Haim Ginott, **Between Parent and Teenager**

Parenting is a stage of growth in life. It can be a form of freedom, of liberation from selfishness to selflessness, leading to an experience of joy. *Joy in Parenting* provides an opportunity for you, as a parent, to learn skills to become a "better" parent and to experience "Joy in Parenting."

Goals include becoming more confident as a parent, understanding your child better, learning alternatives to spanking and nagging when disciplining, learning to handle your emotions and feelings and helping your child to do the same, learning to develop your child as a sexual being, learning how to teach him values and learning how to enjoy your child as a parent. This book provides an opportunity for you to learn how to parent your child through work sheets at the end of each unit.

To enjoy being a parent, you must know your child. It is important to watch and listen to him as he is telling you so much about himself.

Observing and listening will provide information to help you become more aware of your child's growth stages and individual personality patterns. Each child is an individual with hidden talents that we as parents can help develop if we know what they are.

You will become more aware of your relationship with your child and his relationship with others. A well-working and happy relationship with your child is more important than what approach you use with him as long as extreme methods of teaching are not used. This relationship will serve as a model for his relationship with others.

By observing and listening to your child, he will give you a clearer picture of how he sees himself and how he relates to the real world around him. He needs a positive self-image to think well of himself. Only after thinking well of himself can he feel good about other people.

Observations will provide a way for you and his teacher to exchange ideas. Communication with personnel at the school your child attends is a must if you are to help him grow in all areas of development.

You will find out that you have joys and concerns in common with other parents. It helps to share these joys and concerns by attending parenting classes, reading child development books and participating in discussion groups. Sharing is part of a basic human need and will help us build our confidence as parents.

By observing your child, you will become more aware of your child's strengths and the areas in which he needs help. By knowing strengths, we can praise and provide opportunity for development. By knowing areas that need more help, we can guide and serve as examples. In order to guide, we need knowledge. We spend years preparing for a trade or profession but so little time on being a parent. Parenting is not instinct, it is a learned skill.

What should I observe about my child? Conversations denote communication. While working on a special area with your child, jot down your conversations. It is best to keep paper and pencil handy, on the TV set or on the refrigerator. We forget so easily. If he is acting negatively, you may see a pattern evolving that will help you understand why he is acting as he does.

Write down conversations you may hear between your child and other children. His feelings will be verbalized in play situations and give you a better idea of his actions. Record conversations between your child and other adults. How he reacts to them and his feeling toward them will be noticed in his conversations with them.

Observe and listen to how the child responds to various activities in the home. Is he cooperative or unwilling or noncommital? How does he respond to other children? Is he aggressive or shy? Notice how he responds to other adults outside the family.

You need to consider when you see growth or why you think he acts like he does. What problems do you see or what questions do you have? When you know these problems and questions, you can begin to work on them. If you can't solve them yourself, professional help is available. Mental Health Clinics in your area provide such services through counselors, psychologists and psychiatrists. Schools also can recommend proper sources of help for a particular problem. Welfare agencies, such as Children Services, as well as educational sources in the form of parenting classes sponsored by Adult Education or Parks and Recreation in your community provide help for parents. County Health Departments provide endless information concerning the health of your child. Churches provide valuable counseling through priests, sisters and ministers.

Perhaps the problem cannot be solved now but will be in a later period of growth. For example, temper tantrums are common for the pre-schooler and tend to dissolve into more subtle ways of achieving a desired goal, such as verbal rebellion in the older child. Educators and psychologists, such as Piaget, tell us to study the child to find out what concepts he can conceive at a given age and then teach him the material he can grasp at the time. Only then do we have the idealistic learning experience.

Observe your child's play interests, fun-times or hobbies. What does he think of himself? His ability to share will promote social growth. Is he influenced easily by others? Children who do not think well of themselves or have a low self-esteem are more easily influenced by others. Can he manage his own affairs? By giving him responsibility, he will learn to do so. Observe his attitudes toward limits set in the home. How does he respond to them? What about attitudes toward those in authority, such as his teachers? Observe attitudes toward learning in general. What are his attitudes toward his peers?

What are his fears and cautions? Does he have control over them or do they control him? Lastly, observe his attitudes toward you as his parent and the home life he lives in.

Certainly we cannot observe all day long or every day. But when you are working on a particular growth pattern, it is worth the effort to do some research and then work from there. As parents we cannot work on assumptions. You will be well rewarded as you see progress in the growth pattern you are working on.

Remember that parents are not perfect. We all make mistakes. Children are sturdy. If love is a bond between parent and child, mistakes can be a learning situation. The past is over. Begin now. Put parenting skills to work and do the best you can. Put aside guilt feelings and enjoy your vocation as a parent.

To help each family member get to know one another better, try the following activity: have each person draw a picture of your family in a favorite activity. It is not necessary to draw figures. You may use colors, circles or lines, to denote each member of the family. Take the time for each one to explain his favorite family activity. Listen and observe. Joy is a happening.

You have loved me,
I have bloomed

SELF ESTEEM, PARENT & CHILD

SELF-ESTEEM

"Self-esteem is the mainspring that slates every child for success or failure as a human being."

Dorothy Briggs, **Your Child's Self Esteem**

Self-esteem is how your child feels about himself. How he feels about himself will determine the friends he chooses, how he gets along with his peers and adults, and how productive he will be in life.

Our children reflect what we are. We are the models through which our children learn to value themselves. As parents, we need to increase our self-acceptance to be more accepting of the child. How do we feel about ourselves? Take a piece of paper and pencil. Draw a line down the middle. On one side list what you like about yourself. On the other side list what you don't like about yourself. Which list is longer? Look at the list of "don't likes." Is what you don't like about yourself something you can or can't change? If it can be changed, you need to start working. If it can't, you need to accept this about yourself. For example, perhaps you are uncomfortable in groups of peers. This can be worked on with gradual exposure, encouragement and practice role-play situations. But if you are unhappy with the physical appearance of your nose, and plastic surgery is out of the question due to expense, you need to live with this situation and "make the most" of it.

If we feel good about ourselves, we will not act aggressively, violating the rights of others. Neither will we act passively, giving in to everyone. On a continuum line of passive, assertive, aggressive, self-esteem would be how an assertive person feels about himself. To be assertive, one respects himself as well as others. This means feeling good about oneself and others.

Let's pretend you are in a restaurant and order a steak medium-rare and it comes to you well-done. What would be your reaction? A passive person would eat the steak even though it is not what he wants. He would not think well enough of himself to send back the steak. The aggressive person, however, would make a scene sending his steak back, intruding on the privacy of other diners and perhaps verbally abusing the waitress. Aggressiveness usually expresses low self-esteem. The assertive person, or one who feels good about himself, would send his steak back quietly and ask for what he ordered, a medium-rare steak. When we help our children develop a positive self-image, we will help them become more assertive.

Who am I? All of us have three important personality ego states: parent, adult and child. The parent in us acts as a tape, playing back our reactions to our parents' teachings. A husband asked his wife why she cut the ends of the roast off before she put it in the pan. "Mother always did that," was the reply. So when mother came to visit, he asked the question again. Grandma replied, "Because the roast wouldn't fit in the pan." A person with too much parent is quite bossy and mothering.

The adult is our reasoning ego. "I'd like to have that new car. It's beautiful, but it costs too much. We need the money for Jim's education." A person with too much adult in his personality can be very analytical.

The child ego state is important. This makes the daily routine of life bearable. We have the job of watering the yard, but what fun to turn the hose on ourselves on such a hot day! A person with too much child in his personality can be irresponsible or unreliable, for example, not showing up on time for an appointment.

What kind of a person are you? Too much parent or child or adult? The stage of life we are in may accentuate one of these stages of personality. People's behavior can trigger an ego state in us. If someone approaches us in his child ego state, we may react in a parent ego state. "I don't want to go to work today." "Don't be silly, you might be fired and we can't afford that. You go!"

Even a very young child has these three ego states in his personality. Did you ever see a four-year-old mothering a crying child? The parent state is being expressed. A four-year-old who puts a puzzle together is acting in the adult state. A four-year-old having a temper tantrum is in his child ego state.

Do you basically enjoy being yourself or would you rather be someone else? There are times we all would rather be someone else. This is a normal feeling. A person who thinks well of himself accepts himself for what he is and tries to capitalize on his strong points, not his weaknesses. Think about what you do especially well. Perhaps it's working with wood or creative cooking. It is not important what it is that you do well, just so you recognize that there is something that you do well.

If you are a worthwhile and lovable person, then you are important enough to make time for yourself. Do you make time for yourself? Maybe it's a half hour a day away from everyone just doing what you want to do: reading a book, going for a walk or taking a bubble bath. How do you make time for yourself? What do you do for yourself?

Formulating goals in life is an important part of developing positive self-esteem. Where am I going? Have I formulated goals for my life? Are my goals realistic? Goals need to be challenging but they must be attainable. It is better to have fewer goals that are attainable than many that cannot be fulfilled. Start with daily goals. Make a list of four or five goals, and as they are accomplished cross them out. This will give you a feeling of success and let you feel good about yourself. If you cannot accomplish this many, cut the list back or, if they are easily completed, increase the number.

You will need goals for the role of life you are playing now, being a parent for example. A parent of young children will have different goals than a parent of teenagers.

Major goals of parenting might include education, teaching moral values. fulfilling basic emotional and physical needs. More specific goals for education would be helping a child learn numbers and colors, or providing experiences, such as a family camping trip, for him to learn and store for school learning.

It is important to remember that self-esteem is learned. Low self-image can be changed to high self-image. This may take effort and perhaps a change in environment, but it can be done. The younger the child, the easier it is to change. There are many factors that influence self-esteem. The environment we live, work and play in helps to determine our self-image. What people say to us or about us is important. We are concerned about how our neighbors and friends feel about us. We tend to avoid people who never have anything nice to say to us, or about us to others. We can feel hurt or rejected and not very capable or lovable. If people we live and work with think highly of us, then we will think highly of ourselves. A husband or wife who encourages us will make us feel good about ourselves. When we receive a thank-you or a compliment for putting forth effort, we feel good about ourselves.

Culture and tradition consist of attitudes of men toward women and women toward men. How we feel about being married and our marriage relationship stem from our "upbringing." Attitudes toward sex contribute greatly toward how we feel about our bodies and ourselves. Prejudices are learned and circumscribe many facets of life, from food to people. Religion is a base for many attitudes that form high or low self-image. Our vision of God as a stern disciplinarian, or as a loving father, can affect how we feel about ourselves and our relationships with others.

Formal learning influences self-esteem. How we progress in school, our teachers attitudes toward us, what we like to do and our life work are all attributed to learning experiences. A teacher who ridicules your art paper in front of the class might discourage you from enjoying art activities the rest of your life. On the other hand, patience, praise and encouragement make you feel capable and willing to try again.

The family plays the most important role in forming self-images. By the age of five the child has deep roots of high or low self-esteem. The way parents talk to their children, how they touch them and what body language they use flash images to their children. Children are persons and need to be treated with dignity. At times, if we talked to our friends the way we talk to our children, we wouldn't have many friends.

The media, especially television, influence self-esteem. A tv program like *The Waltons* or *Little House on the Prairie* might give us feelings of failure as a parent. Our experiences with our family do not always turn out so perfectly. We need to take these programs for what they are—entertainment and not a lifestyle. Children spend many hours watching tv. They are forming self-images through models portrayed in television shows instead of "real life" models. We need to help provide those models for our children as they move away from us into the world.

Children form self-images from parents in many ways. Words are important tools used to create high self-esteem. Pretend you are a child—about seven years old. How do you feel when your mother says the following statement to you? "Get out of here. I don't want to talk to you now. You always bother me when I'm busy," or, "I just showed you how to do that. You're so stupid, nothing sinks in. Why do you have to be so dumb?" or, "I know you like to use my pen, and I'd like to let you use it, but you need to ask before you do as I have spent a lot of time looking for it." The first statement probably doesn't make you feel very good about yourself. Do you feel rejected? If your parents don't want you, who does? The second statement is labeling you "stupid" and "dumb." Those names certainly do not make one feel capable. The last statement shows concern and interest for you—not that what you do is approved, but you are being spoken to with respect.

Be sure your child is listening to you before you talk. How do you know when he is listening to you? Eye contact is important but does not always assure listening is happening. Body language will help to tell you if your child is listening. Watch for facial expressions. Your child's response will determine if he has been listening to you. Your body-presence, standing next to your child, will invite his attention. Eye-level is very effective in communication. Try this experiment. Stand next to a partner who is sitting down. Begin a conversation, then after a few minutes switch places and continue talking. How did you feel standing while trying to carry on a conversation with someone sitting down? Did you feel in command? Uncomfortable looking down? Did you want to sit down? What about when you were sitting? Did you feel inferior? Did your neck begin to hurt as you kept looking up? Did you want to stand, or end the conversation quickly? If your child is small, get down to his eye level. If he is six feet tall, sit down at a table to talk. You'll both feel more comfortable.

Try not to be judgmental while you are listening. Listen and answer back in a supportive manner that will open communication rather than close it: "You sound very upset at what your brother did" rather than "I don't care how you feel. Don't you ever speak to your brother like that again."

While listening you are able to hear many more words than are spoken. That is why your mind begins to wander no matter how hard you try to concentrate. Your child also is easily distracted. Reinforce his listening ability by using the above techniques.

Use positive phraseology when talking to children. Instead of "don't," be positive: "You need to. . . .", "It's time to. . . .", "This is the way we do it at our home." "Do you need some help?", "I would like you to help me do this." These phrases result in far more positive feelings and behavior than: "Don't do that." "Can't you hear?" "I don't care what the teacher said, can't you do anything right?'' "Can't you ever do anything you are told?'' Discard from your vocabulary words like: good, bad, nice, naughty, etc. These words label. When a child is labeled, he lives up to his label. Constantly calling a child "sloppy" will help the child remain sloppy. He gets attention when he performs in this manner. His self-esteem can be lowered to the point of his feeling, "What is the use of trying?'' Remember, it is the action we are displeased with; the room is sloppy, the drawers are sloppy, not the child. Label the action, not the child. Constantly calling the child "good" may set a goal too high for the child to reach. How much better it is to say, "I like the way you followed the rules," instead of, "You're such a good girl."

When you tell a child how you feel about what he has done, it helps to begin with the word "I." As soon as you say "I" you will turn attention to your feelings, rather than labeling. "I am very upset with the way you keep this room. It looks sloppy and nothing can be found." Compare this to "You're sloppy. You keep this room like a pigpen." Can you feel the difference? The first statement tells the child how you feel. Parents have a right to their feelings. A child needs to know this. The statement is attacking the action. The second statement attacks the very being of the child and helps to form low self-esteem. No one can feel good after being called sloppy. This puts the child on the defensive and he will want to fight back. However, he won't want to fight back if you are expressing your feelings. He may surprise you by showing some concern for your feelings. "I'm sorry Mom. I didn't think this would upset you so much."

Be generous with your words of praise. Praise is a social reinforcer. We all need reinforcement for acts performed. If we desire a certain behavior, we need to reinforce it. Nagging tends to reinforce negative behavior. Praise is recognition of achievement. Whenever your child behaves in a manner acceptable to you, praise him. "I'm pleased you learned how to do that. I feel good when you follow through on what I ask you to do." Praise can be used to follow failure. Imagine that you're a child for a moment. You have been working very hard trying to learn to tie your shoelace. You feel frustrated, ready to give up. It's just too difficult. Then Dad says, "I like the way you're trying. You almost have it. Let me show you an easier way." Now your feelings have changed. "Dad will help. I'll try again." Contrast this to, "Quit asking me to help you. I've showed you a million times. You're just too dumb to learn." It is better to stop trying than to be called dumb. If our words communicate love, concern, encouragement, acceptance, sensitivity and understanding, we will be developing capable and lovable feelings in our children—in other words, developing high self-esteem. Resulting from this communication will be success, achievement, creativity, interest, cooperation, curiosity and enthusiasm. If our words communicate ridicule, sarcasm, rejection, annoyance, distrust, discouragement and impatience we can expect aggression, failure, withdrawal, tension, hostility, fear, guilt and submissiveness. Our words will be communicating a sense of failure or low self-esteem.

Body language has come into prominence in recent years. The expression on our faces, the position of our hands or legs can tell our children so much. "Yes, you can go," said with a smile can come across meaning, "Go, and have a good time." If the same words are said with clenched teeth and fists, the message that comes across is "I'm sick of your nagging. Go and get out of here." Your body needs to reflect what your words say for a message to be effective. If they conflict, the child will respond to the body language. He will be confused by the double message you are sending. Unfortunately, we cannot see ourselves when we are talking to others. Try this little experiment. Stand in front of a mirror and imagine you are talking to your child without saying a word. He has just done something to make you very angry. Perhaps he tracked mud all across your kitchen floor. Show him you are angry. Remember, no words. Now, show him how happy you are. He has just handed you a bouquet of flowers. Try looking surprised. He cleaned his room without you telling him to do so. Now do the same actions again, this time using words. Do your facial expressions and words match? If they do, you are communicating your feelings effectively. Your child will not be confused by a double message.

How children are physically treated has a great deal to do with how they form self-esteem. Gentle touches, hugs and kisses make a child feel wanted, loved and capable. As your child gets older he may not appreciate a kiss, especially in front of peers, but straightening his shirt or blouse is acceptable, showing you care. I'm sure you have all observed a child in a grocery store, being dragged by his arm. The more the parent pulls, the more the child screams; the more the child screams, the more he is dragged along. The child cannot feel worthwhile being dragged along. It must be very uncomfortable. Pulling, shoving, pinching or pushing, as well as slapping, lower his self-esteem and dignity.

Children feel good about themselves if they can experience mastery and achievement. That "success" feeling that we all know so well is important in helping us to feel capable and good about ourselves. Goals we set for our children and goals they set for themselves will help determine if they will have feelings of success or failure. Children need challenges, but they need challenges they can meet. A child who is working to capacity and earns C's in school will not know the meaning of success if you expect A's. He will constantly experience failure in your eyes and give up. Study your child. Set goals that are realistic to him and for the stage of growth and development he is in. Make home the most important place to him. An easier place to live in can feature, for example, a bench to stand on in the bathroom, easy storage for toys, lower racks for towels, etc. By being able to do things for himself, he will have a feeling of capability.

Children develop self-image by our example. They learn by imitating. If we feel good about ourselves, this will radiate to them. How we handle ourselves in daily life with our family, friends and business acquaintances will teach our children to handle their interactions with people. Communicating in an assertive manner, realizing our needs and fulfilling them in a way that is not aggressive, or intruding on others, or passive or submissive to others, will teach our children to do the same. Being assertive is a sign of high self-esteem. That is feeling good about oneself.

It is easier for children to feel good about themselves if their basic needs are met. Your child needs to have his physical needs satisfied. Good nutrition, plenty of rest and fresh air, physical exercise and shelter are needed. These are usually obvious to parents and taken care of. When a child feels good physically, he can begin to feel good about himself.

Emotional needs are more difficult to fulfill. Every child needs to feel he is loved, most importantly by those closest to him. Being rejected by a casual acquaintance is quite a bit different than being rejected by a parent.

He needs to feel capable. By giving him responsibility appropriate for his age, teaching him to make decisions, letting him experience the consequences of his actions and giving him "success" experiences, he will feel capable in life. He needs to learn early that he can't "squeeze water from a stone," that if one person does not love him, he can find appropriate love elsewhere.

Your child needs to feel important. Letting him be a part of the family by being in on making rules, deciding chores, planning outings, etc., will help him to feel important. Teaching him skills in many areas of living will help him to feel confident in himself.

All his life he will need to interact with people. Teach him to do this at an early age. Let him experience disappointments as they happen. Express your feelings to him so he knows it's all right to be angry and to say so; what is important in relationships with people is how he channels that anger.

Teaching him to say thank you, and please, will make life more pleasant for people around him. If he learns respect for others and their property, he will be pleased in return by the respect others will show him.

Enjoy and appreciate your child. You will teach him to appreciate and enjoy others. Thank him for the little things he does for you—picking a flower for you, cleaning the garage, fixing that broken shelf. Look for these things and show him how much you appreciate them. Have fun with your child. Laugh with him, watch a sunset, watch the ants while they carry food to their nest. Throw pebbles into the creek and watch the water ripple. See who can count the most ripples. Remember, not only are you enjoying your child, you are building his self-image and helping him learn to enjoy others.

Your teenager feels good about himself. But you have just moved into a new neighborhood. How will he react? Of course, he will miss his old friends, but with your encouragement he will try to approach and talk to classmates in his new school. He will want to ask a friend over. If he is disappointed in his peers reaction to him, he will express this disappointment to the family and together you can come up with another approach that will help him try again. If your teenager does not feel good about himself, he will tend to sulk around the house. He may be very uncooperative and show angry feelings toward you for making him move. He may refuse to move, or may even run away. What can you as a parent do to help him? Invite a family over with children his age, volunteer to help with the group at school, such as transportation to a game. By getting the children together they are bound to communicate. Let him take a vacation for a week or so, if possible, back with his friends where you lived before. Plan a party with him, or an outing to the lake with several other families. You may need to provide opportunities for him to feel confident once again.

Your three year old is left with a baby-sitter. He is very unhappy and cries most of the evening making it difficult for the baby-sitter. What can you as a parent do to make him feel more confident when you're gone? Perhaps a special planned activity for your child and the baby-sitter to do together would help. Playdough, made especially for the night, would be a treat. Fingerpainting is great fun; a new story for the baby-sitter to read, or a new record for them to listen to will help. By his seeing you return each time, a trust relationship is building between you and your child. Your having a "matter-of-fact" attitude about leaving will help. Never sneak out; it will frighten the child more. As your child becomes more confident in himself and develops high self-esteem, he will be able to be separated from you for longer periods of time.

Have every member of your family make a collage. This will help you to better know each other, and you will have a good time doing it. Take old magazines and cut, or tear out pictures that reflect your likes and aspirations, foods you enjoy, sports you like, clothes you like; colors that are you, and ideas that shout "you" can make up your collage. Paste them in any order you like on a large sheet of paper. When you are done, each family member takes turns talking about the pictures that represent themselves. This is an excellent way for each of you to begin to look at each other.

Self-esteem is vital in our daily living. Researchers tell us that self-image determines who our friends are, the life work we choose, the kind of marriage we will have and the type of parents we will be. You are a determining factor in building your child's self-esteem. Enjoy yourself and your child so he can learn to enjoy himself and you.

DEVELOPING HIGH SELF-ESTEEM IN MYSELF

"Each person values himself to the degree that he has been valued."
Dorothy Corkille Briggs, **Your Child's Self-Esteem**

Take time to be alone. Get to know yourself. Answering the following questions will help you to know how you feel about yourself.

— Who am I?

— What kind of person am I?

— Do I basically enjoy being myself or would I rather be someone else?

— What do I do that I know I do especially well?

— Do I think I am important enough to have time for myself?

— Do I make time for myself?

— How do I make time for myself?

— What do I do for myself?

— What do I like about myself?

— Is what I don't like about myself something I can or can't change?

— How do I feel when I receive compliments?

— Are compliments I receive in those areas I am working hardest to change the ones that please me the most?

— Do I need people around me all the time?

— Do I accept projects to be popular, because I enjoy them, or because they have to be done?

— Do I make impossible demands on myself?

— Where am I going?

— Have I formulated goals for my life? What are they at this present state of my life?

— Are my goals realistic?

Remember—a low self-esteem is acquired. It can be changed.

SELF-ESTEEM

Buzz Questions

1. Think back as early as you can remember to a situation or a person that made you feel good about yourself. What happened? Who was involved? What was the result?

2. Think back as early as you can remember to a situation or a person that did not make you feel good about yourself. What happened? Who was involved? What was the result?

3. Which is easier to recall, the positive or negative experience? Why do you think this is so?

COMMUNICATION THAT DEVELOPS
A POSITIVE SELF-IMAGE

The most effective communication is simple, slow, direct and given in a moderate tone. Facial expression and body language need to coincide with spoken words.

- Make certain the child is listening.
- Use a vocabulary that the child understands.
- Lowering pitch and decreasing speed and volume make communication more effective.
- For better results, give series of directions one at a time, or in order of expected performance according to age and ability.

LISTENING is actively hearing and trying to understand your child's message.

1. Be attentive.
2. Stop your activity.
3. Look at your child on his eye level.
4. Observe his body language: sad face, drooping posture, bright smile.
5. Repeat to your child what you hear him saying. "It sounds like you ...". This will help the child understand his feelings.
6. Be non-judgmental. Help the child form his own judgment.

USE positive language. Instead of "don't," be positive. Tell him what he cannot do, the reason why, and what he can do. Example: "I cannot let you jump on the couch. You may hurt yourself and I cannot pay for a new couch. You may jump on your jumping board." These are some phrases that should become part of your vocabulary:

"You need to _____."
"This is the way we do at our house."
"It is time to _____."
"This is a place to _____."
"Your hands need to be helped."
"I should like you to help me do this."
"Do you need some help?"
"If you cannot come by yourself, I will help you."
"I think you are able to do it without help."
"It sounds better when _____."

DISCARD from your vocabulary: good, bad, nice, naughty, big, sloppy, shy, dumb, brat, etc.

Avoid labeling your child. Children live up to labels. Labeling lowers self-image. Talk about the act, not the child.

Instead of "good" or "nice" try "You have learned how to _____," or "That is the right way to do it." Or, "You did that very well." Instead of, "Now be a good boy," try "Have a good time." Being labeled "good" is very difficult to live up to. Guilt feelings can evolve from this. A child cannot be good all the time.

Instead of "bad" or "naughty" try "You haven't learned how to _____,"
or "When you have learned enough, you won't do _____,"
or "I don't like what you did." Disapprove the act, not the child. Instead of, "What a big girl you are to do that," try "You have learned a lot about _____,"
or "You know how now, don't you?"

PRAISE is a word, phrase or gesture that makes another person feel good about himself. It helps a child have a sense of well-being. He will want to repeat the behavior that instigates praise.

1. Praise should follow the act as soon as possible to be effective.
2. Praise should not contain negative comments. For example: "I'm happy you remembered to empty the trash. I hope you don't forget to do it tomorrow."
3. Praise the act, not the child's character. "The room is really a mess," not, "Boy, are you sloppy."
4. Praise can follow failure to encourage effort: "I liked the way you tried." You can add, "Let me show you an easier way to do this."
5. Be specific when you praise. Instead of, "You did a fine job." — "I like the way you raked the leaves and put them in such neat piles. Thanks, that helped me a lot."

Use "I" instead of "YOU" to gain cooperation from your child and to help him feel better about himself.

1. When something happens that bothers you, say the word "I" first. This will help you to express your feelings. Your feelings are your own and no one can argue with you about them. Your child will learn that it is all right to feel angry, disappointed, sad, happy, etc.
2. Saying "I" first, also will prevent you from labeling and name calling. After expressing your feelings, take care of the matter at hand. "I'm furious at this mess! You need to clean it up right now! You may not go out with your friend until this is cleaned up." You expressed your feelings, told the child what had to be done, and the consequences that would follow if the mess wasn't cleaned up.
3. "You make me!" "You always!" "You never!" all shut off communication by putting the child on the defensive. He learns to turn you off.

WAYS TO PRAISE CHILDREN

I like the way you shared your bicycle.

You're doing a good job of waiting in line.

You're walking nicely.

You did a fine job making your bed.

I'm happy you did what I asked you to do.

That is an excellent answer.

You're being very careful with that glass of milk.

I like what you said—that's well thought out.

You have been such a helpful worker.

That's good planning for having a pet.

You are a careful thinker; you think before you speak.

You couldn't have said it or have done it better.

It looks like you're putting some thought and time into this.

You remembered all the rules. I'm proud of you.

Thank you for listening to my question.

It's nice to see you helping each other.

I'm happy that you listened to me.

I like the way you are working.

I like the way you tried. Let me show you an easier way.

You did a fine job handling your anger toward that frustrating work.

Thank you for doing more of the clean-up of your room than you had to.

You really did a fine job playing with your brother.

It's a pleasure to work with you.

I like it when you look at me while I'm talking to you.

I like such pleasant conversations with you.

That's good table manners to wipe your mouth with your napkin.

I knew you could do that well.

You have your thinking cap on today.

That was a grown-up thing to do.

You are 100 percent correct.

DEVELOPING HIGH SELF-ESTEEM IN MY CHILD

Self-esteem is how your child feels about himself. When basic needs are met, self-esteem is higher.

EVERY CHILD NEEDS TO FEEL LOVABLE:
The expression on your face, your body language and the tone of your voice should give him that feeling.
Show an interest in things that are important to him.
Remember what it was like to be a child and see things from his point of view.
Take time to listen and talk to your child and encourage him to communicate with you.
Take time to enjoy being his parent.

EVERY CHILD NEEDS TO FEEL WORTHWHILE:
Look at your child when you talk to him. Talk to him at eye level and use words he understands.
Your child will know you love him even when you are too busy to stop to talk if you tell him you will be with him as soon as possible, and you remember to do so.
Do not compare your child unfavorably with his brothers and sisters or friends.
Do not try to satisfy your own ambitions through his achievements.
Provide opportunities for your child to grow independently by giving him responsibility and privileges as he earns them.

EVERY CHILD NEEDS TO FEEL SUCCESS:
Recognize your child's effort with praise given sincerely.
Put goals within his reach.
Recognize that your child must have some challenging goals.
Let him feel the satisfaction of his own accomplishments.

EVERY CHILD NEEDS TO FEEL IMPORTANT:

Discuss with your child things which are important to you as a family.

Help your child feel confidence in himself by praising him for jobs well done, and by helping him learn through his mistakes.

Value your child's opinion and give it consideration.

Help him learn to carry his share of responsibility as a family member.

Appreciate and enjoy your child so he can appreciate and enjoy others.

EVERY CHILD NEEDS TO LEARN TO INTERACT WITH PEOPLE:

Give your child opportunity to meet people outside of the family.

Help him to adjust to disappointments.

Help your child develop skills in many areas of living.

Give him examples of courtesy and consideration for others.

SELF-ESTEEM

Buzz Questions

1. How does a child who feels confident behave in the following situations:
   Being sent to the store to buy something?
   Moving to a new neighborhood?
   Being left with a babysitter?

2. How does a child who does not feel confident behave in the above situations?

3. What can you do as a parent to help your child feel more confident in the above situations?

OBSERVATION ON SELF-ESTEEM

Self-esteem is how one values oneself. The family is the prime determinant of how we feel about ourselves. How we feel about ourselves, in turn, determines how we feel about others, and about life itself.

1. During the week, observe what activities and events may have contributed positively to your child's self-esteem. Example: made a new friend.

2. Did any events occur during the week which might have lowered your child's self-value? Examples: a) rejection from another child, b) an angry criticism from his mother because of dawdling, or c) father, while reading newspaper pretends to listen to child.

3. What characteristics do you observe about your child which show he feels good about himself? For example: facial expressions, posture, etc.

4. What characteristics do you observe when your child is not feeling good about himself?

5. List positive words which you feel describe your child.

"REAL"

"What is *real*?" asked the Calico Rabbit one day when they were lying side by side on the floor in the corner of the nursery before Nana came to tidy the room. "Does it mean having things inside you that buzz, and a stick-out handle?"

"Really, it isn't how you're made," said the Gingham Horse. "It's a thing that *HAPPENS* to you. When a child loves you for a long time, not just to play with, but *REALLY* loves you, then you become REAL."

"Does it hurt," asked the Rabbit.

"Sometimes," said the Gingham Horse, for he was always truthful. "But when you are real," he continued, "you don't mind being hurt."

"Does it happen all at once like being wound up," asked the rabbit, "or bit by bit?"

"It doesn't happen all at once," said the Gingham Horse. "You *become.* It takes a long time. That's why it often doesn't happen to people who break easily, or have sharp edges, or who have to be carefully kept. Generally, by the time you are *real*, most of your hair has been loved off and your eyes drop out and you get loose in the joints and very shabby. But these things don't matter at all, because once you're real you can't be ugly, except to people who don't understand."

"I suppose you are real?" said the rabbit. And then he wished he had not said it, for he thought the Gingham Horse might be sensitive. But the Horse only smiled.

"The boy's uncle made me Real," he said. "That was a great many years ago; but once you are *real*, you can't become unreal again. It lasts for always."

The Rabbit sighed. He thought it would be a long time till this magic called REAL happened to him. He longed to become real, to know what it felt like; and yet the idea of growing shabby and losing his eyes and whiskers was rather sad. He wished that he could have it without these uncomfortable things happening to him.

Margery Williams, **The Velveteen Rabbit**

NOTES

Please be patient,
God isn't finished with me

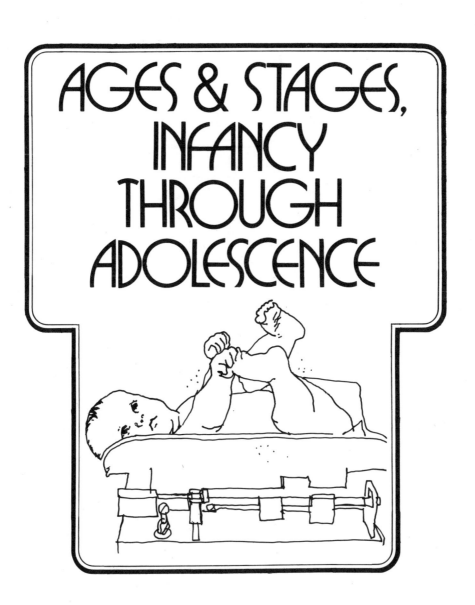

AGES & STAGES,
INFANCY
THROUGH
ADOLESCENCE

AGES AND STAGES

"And He advanced in wisdom and age and grace before God and men."

Luke 2:52

Every child is composed of an intellect, a physical body, and emotions and feelings. He is a sexual being searching for his identity as a male or female, and he has an awareness of a "power" beyond him. He develops in ages and stages, each having its joys and uncomfortable feelings.

Example and imitation play an important role as a child develops maturity. Parents are the first models children imitate. Our mannerisms, habits and ways of doing things are expressed by our children. Watch your preschooler at play. See if you see yourself there somewhere. I can well remember observing two preschoolers playing house in one of my classes. The little girl was busy making dinner and soon ordered the little boy to sit down and eat dinner. He obligingly did so and exclaimed with gusto, "Don't tell me you are serving me this crap again." Amen.

Other exposures are influencing your child as he grows. Television plays an important role in his imitating process. Trying to fly like a favorite hero is a great play pastime for preschoolers. The "Fonzie" rage has engulfed teenagers. Language used in programs is imitated. Research shows that children are becoming violence orientated as they passively sit, hour after hour, watching reoccurring violent scenes on television.

As the child goes off to school, teachers play an important role in the imitating process. Once, while teaching a fourth grade class, I wore a scarf pinned around my neck. Within the next week I noticed all the little girls wore similar scarves styled the same way as mine. Later, talking with parents, it was mentioned to me how the children wanted to imitate everything I did, including my dress. I was overwhelmed at the responsibility that was mine—to serve as an example to twenty-five nine and ten year olds.

As a child enters the preadolescent and adolescent stages we see the peer group as the example to follow. Dress, hair styles, mannerisms, behavior patterns are all modeled after the group. There is a sense of security for the teenager to "belong" to a peer group. This also is an important step in growth; to find out, "Who am I? Where am I going?"

Friends, neighbors, relatives and other adults influence imitative patterns. An uncle may become a hero to imitate, or a good friend of the family who is around quite a bit may serve as an example. All these models will eventually be sorted out by the child as he searches for the "real me."

There are facts about growth patterns of children that parents need to know. Children are all individuals and need to learn at the rate they are capable. Comparisons with other children, siblings, and friends should be avoided. It is so easy to say, "Why can't you keep your room as neatly as your sister does?" or "Your brother knew how to do that a long time ago." Your child is an individual, a unique person. There is no one else like him in the world. Handle his development individually. "I'm upset with the way your room is kept." or "I'm happy you learned how to do that." All children cannot excel in the same area. We need to find our children's talents and capitalize on these. Each child can do something well. Look for it and praise him.

Children need to go through all stages of development without being pushed ahead or kept behind. Forcing a young child to read when he is not ready can cause damaging effects later on. Holding a child back from growing socially can keep a teenager from emancipation and tie him emotionally to his family for a lifetime.

Toilet training is one area where parents tend to push their children ahead, probably because of convenience. As an adult, it is not important when you were "potty trained." Job applications do not require that information. We need to be realistic about when the child is ready and then guide him from there. Forcing a child may cause low self-esteem if he does not feel capable or lovable.

Listen to your child, observe him, and when you feel he is ready for a new step, then begin to teach him. If he is having difficulty with it, stop for awhile, then reteach him. See if he is ready at that time. He needs to be challenged, but he needs to be challenged in a way that he can feel successful.

When there is progression in learning, we must remember that there may also be regression. Bedwetting may start again at six. An eight year old may have temper tantrums again. These are only a temporary setbacks if properly handled. Patience and understanding are needed. Reteach again. Severe punishment only causes the child to regress further. Try to find out what caused this setback. Is it physical? Was there a crisis in the family? Is the child experiencing an emotional trauma? If properly handled, this will be the forerunner of a new growth stage.

Somewhere around four, the child is deeply involved in the imaginary stage. He may carry around an imaginary friend or, as one parent told me, a whole boy scout troop. Remember the friend is his and not yours. When your child wants to set a place at the table for his imaginary friend, let him. You do not have to set the place setting. Comments such as "Isn't it fun to pretend?" will help your child to begin to distinguish between what is real and what is imaginary. It is so easy to accuse a child of lying when he exclaims, "There is a green monster under my bed," or "a pink elephant in the backyard." He is trying to cope with his feelings, perhaps fear of the dark. Not being able to explain his fear, he will express it with an imaginary object. Help him face his feelings. Try to find out what he is afraid of and comfort him. A flashlight of his very own under his pillow will help conquer his fear of the dark, rather than saying, "How ridiculous! There is no such animal under your bed. Go to sleep or you will get a spanking." He needs you to be the level between what is real and what is imaginary. When a child can begin to distinguish between what is real and what is imaginary, he is entering a new growth stage.

Curiosity in children needs to be respected as a vital learning procedure. This is one way children learn. When a two year old keeps asking "why" it is usually for attention or imitation. When a four year old asks "why?" he wants to know why. This will take all of your patience. Try to answer simply. If you can't, be honest. Tell him you'll look it up and then do so. This will establish a trust relationship that will be invaluable when he becomes a teenager. The most effective help that you as a parent can give your child to prepare him for school, or during his school years, is to provide many experiences for him. Take him to different places, such as the fire station or police station. Expose him to the library. Listen to music together. Going on camping trips as a family, fishing, and reading books together are all invaluable experiences for your child and will provide background for his learning in school. One of the most meaningful compliments I ever received was from a teacher who told me that my child had a wealth of experiences to share with his class. He never lacked material to write about.

Children think concretely. They see situations as black and white, not shades of gray. Abstract thinking comes later, about the ages of twelve or thirteen for some children. Concepts of algebra being taught in 7th and 8th grade might be learned by some, but by many is memorizing with little understanding. Abstract concepts are beginning to take root at this time. History isn't taught until the upper grades because it is an abstract subject. In the primary grades, the family and immediate community are studied because the child is living here and now and can accept this learning.

Educators and psychologists tell us that it is important to understand the concepts children are capable of having at a given age level for the most effective learning to take place. To teach a third grader intricate facts of American history would be a waste of time and effort. Some memorization might take place, but no real understanding of the material. Expecting your two year old to understand that he may not touch that vase on the table because it is valuable is a waste of time, but your ten year old can begin to understand the quality of the vase and can begin to realize why he must be careful with it.

It is difficult for children to make judgements. "How many times" is more important than "how much." If a child broke two drinking glasses of no significant value and didn't get punished for doing so, he would be surprised. He can't understand why yesterday when he accidentally broke one vase that was valuable, he was severely punished. To a young child at Christmas time, several packages of insignificant value are more impressive than only one package of value. Quantity is more important than quality to children.

Children live in the present. What happened yesterday is of no importance and what will happen tomorrow is of no concern. This is one reason why learning has to be repetitious. Even though you have explained why he could not cross the street alone yesterday, you must explain it again today. As he gets older he will be able to establish relationship between what happened yesterday, what happens today, and what will happen tomorrow.

It is difficult for children to establish relationships. If one is punished for hitting his brother, he may pinch him next time, not seeing the two are related. We need to be specific when we state rules to be followed. It is better to make rules together as a family. They are followed more readily.

Because it is difficult for children to establish relationships, God is a difficult concept for children to understand. He will be pictured as a person. More than likely, it will be the father-image that will determine the child's image of God. Whether the young child sees God as a loving person or strict disciplinarian, or someone to be feared, will depend on how he feels about himself in his family environment and how he feels about members of his family.

Interesting studies were made of children in various locations around the world. These studies showed that children grow and develop mentally and emotionally through their art work in the same pattern, but that they developed at a different rate, according to their learning exposure. For example, children begin by scribbling. Soon shapes develop from the scribbling, such as circles, dots, and rectangles. Around three or four radials appear from the circles and this forms the common sun we see in children's drawings. Eventually, two of the radials are extended and legs are formed. The semblance of a human being is beginning. About five, six, or seven years of age, children progress to make a house with curling smoke coming from the chimney. A skyline is formed with a ground line and everything sits on the bottom line, eventually. Where children have not had guidance and exposure to a learning environment, these stages progressed at a later age. The important point being that all children did eventually progress through the various stages.

We can find joy in our children if we can understand them. Let us begin with preschoolers. Remember that when we say two, three, or four years we are giving you a norm. Children are individuals, no two are alike. Your child may go through a four year old stage at three or at five. You'll need to find where he is in his growth development and guide him from there.

From birth to six years there is tremendous growth that takes place, physically, intellectually, emotionally, socially and spiritually. We know that the infant child is learning very rapidly. By the time the child is one he has progressed physically from laying on his back to rolling over, to sitting up, to crawling and even perhaps, to walking. Intellectually, he begins to follow objects, colors will attract him. He begins to reach out and tries to grab objects and then to pull them toward him and put them in his mouth.

He can taste and feel. He learns that he is a separate entity from his mother. By putting objects to his mouth he learns what is part of him or what is not part of him. When he puts his fingers in his mouth he feels two sensations, those of his mouth and those of his fingers. When he puts someone elses fingers in his mouth he feels only one sensation.

Emotionally, the infant learns when he feels comfortable and when he feels uncomfortable, and he knows how to make those around him fulfill his needs. His cries mean special happenings to his mother. Parents learn early how to distinguish the different cries of their child.

Socially, he begins to recognize faces. By the time he is one, he is a little more cautious of strangers. He knows who mom is, who dad is, and who members of the family are. By nine months of age, a strange face will make him cry.

Spiritually, he is developing by knowing the feeling of love and warmth. These feelings are helping him feel good about himself. This will later help him to feel good about God.

The preschool child is very self-centered. By the time he is two he is going through what we call the "no-no" stage. He has learned the word "no" through imitation and no matter what is asked of him it is "no-no." He is trying to find out who he is and so he is challenging anyone else who interferes with his discovery; he is a separate entity.

The preschooler, from probably about two all the way to school age, is beginning mastery. He is beginning to learn how to do things. When he accomplishes a task, he has a great feeling of success. This is important in developing a positive self-image.

The four year old is very attached to the opposite sexed parent. This is why at times little girls are closely attached to their fathers, and boys follow mother wherever she goes. Here we see signs of the first relationships with the opposite sex. It has been said the four year old is a miniature teenager in this aspect.

The preschooler progresses from solitary to parallel to group play, and uses all three stages throughout life. Before the child is two and one half he'll usually be playing by himself. He will probably treat other persons as he treats his toys. Usually around the age of two and one half or three, the child will progress to parallel play. He will like to have other children around him, but still basically not interact with them. He will play and watch them intently, learning from them. From three on up, the child begins to be involved in group play, whereby he is actively interacting with children. He plays well with boys and girls. As a parent you will see lots of imagination involved in his play.

The preschooler is eager to learn about his body. He will explore it, want to know about the parts and how they work and their names. He learns in general, and is introduced to learning through his senses. He likes to touch, feel, taste, hear and smell. He needs slow, non-pressurized teaching with lots of repetition and love from parents.

From six to thirteen years of age children need to refine their selfness. There is increased mastery of knowledge with reflections from their peers. The move from self to others is happening; but it is very slow.

Six and seven year-olds have difficulty with their peer group relationships. They are more interested in the teacher's approval and will try any method to get it, even if it interferes with the group. Lots of teasing and tattling go on at this age.

From eight to ten children begin to look for a model to follow. Usually they will try to imitate the parent of the same-sex at this age. Girls are looking at their mothers and are interested in what they are doing and how this will relate to themselves as they grow into adulthood. Boys are interested in their father, as male models. They are trying to discover how their fathers' actions are going to relate to them as men someday. They do need warm exposure to the adult of the same sex at this age.

Somewhere around ten or eleven, and older, the child will begin to be interested in the same-sex models outside of the family. This is when hero worshipping becomes very important. Parents will be able to help their children at this age by providing models that they would like to have their children come in contact with.

Encourage the six to thirteen year-old to join groups of his own age. The gang stage becomes very prominent at this time when children like to be among peers. Secrets and whispering take place, and clubs are formed. This helps the child to move away from his family and is very important as he progresses toward adulthood and the time when he must emancipate himself from his family.

The adolescent period is a transition period from child to adult. How many years this takes depends on each individual child's experiences and his environment. The adolescent needs to become independent of his family. He needs to re-evaluate himself, find out who he is and where he is going, and to set goals that are realistic for himself. He needs to establish a healthy relationship with the opposite sex with the idea of choosing a mate for life.

The adolescent works better within democratic discipline. Surveys have shown that the more democratic the discipline, the less rebellion on the part of teenagers. By letting him be a definite part of family decisions, rules and regulations he is less likely to rebel. He also needs to prepare for a self-supporting occupation. Through education and training he needs to develop a skill which will enable him to be financially self-supporting. The teenager also needs to establish a workable and meaningful philosophy of life. This is a questioning time of his life, and he may turn away from all that has been taught him in the matters of values and morals. He needs time to withdraw into himself so that he can begin to determine who he is and where he is going. It has been found that the stronger the personal worth the teenager has, the more secure he will feel as a person in a group. The lower the self-image, the more he will be pressured from his peers. It will be difficult for him to keep his identity.

No wonder the adolescent stage is full of turmoil! Parents need to understand what is happening so they can guide and not force growth. The rebellion on the part of the teenager is necessary to help push him into the world. It is not a reflection on us as we so often think.

Growth stages do not stop when we "become" adults. We go through stages of development until we die. If we are knowledgable about these stages of "crisis" happening to us, we will be better able to understand ourselves and in turn better able to interact with those around us. Usually when there is a crisis period of questioning, it is followed by a surge of growth. Certain times in our life denote a turning inward to ourselves. Emancipation at 18, a new baby in the family, boredom with a job or marriage , or trying to find out who we are or where we are going around the age of 40 are events that cause us to stop and look inward and prepare for new growth. Growth and development happen in ages and stages. It is important to us as parents to know what those stages are and to be aware of the stage our child is in so we can be supportive and guide him. Give your child courage to take these steps of growth, and you will see joy in your child as he sheds his cocoon and becomes a butterfly.

FACTS ABOUT GROWTH STAGES

1. Children need to experience all growth stages. A child who does not crawl will need to be provided with play opportunities to fulfill this growth stage.

2. Children should not be pushed into a growth stage before they are ready, or kept behind when they are ready. Forcing toilet training may be an example of pushing a child ahead. Keeping a teenager from emancipating is holding back a growth stage.

3. With progression in learning there is often regression. An eight year-old may revert back to keeping a room sloppy or a five year-old may wet the bed again. Be patient and re-teach.

4. Any crisis can set back learning. A new baby in the family can result in an older child wetting the bed again.

5. Children need to progress through the imaginative stage of growth. This is usually at its height from two to six years of age and is the forerunner of creativeness.

6. Children are curious. Four year-olds are constantly asking why; so are teenagers. Give your child experiences and expose them to adults as well as other children.

7. Up to about age ten, children learn facts. After ten, they test facts. Be patient and hold to your teachings during the testing period.

8. Children imitate us and learn by our example. They follow what we do more than what we say.

9. Children think concretely, in black and white terms, not abstractly in shades of grey. Because of this concept, history is not taught until the fifth grade; and values are beginning to form in the pre-adolescent stage of growth.

10. Children live in the present, not the past or the future. This is why we need to repeat our teaching. It is difficult for them to make a connection to the past.

11. It is difficult for children to make judgments. It is more important how many times they do something (quantity) than what they do (quality).

12. Children have a difficult time establishing relationships. They may be punished for hitting, so next time they will try pinching.

AGES AND STAGES

Buzz Questions

1. It is said that the four year-old is a teenager in miniature. List ways they are alike. How are they different?

2. The eight year-old goes out to "meet the world." Explain what this means and list ways he does "meet the world."

3. After ten, children test what they have learned. Give examples of how they do this and why.

4. List the characteristics of a thirteen year-old intellectually, physically, emotionally and socially.

AGES AND STAGES

Development of the Infant

Infant to four months—

The infant is startled by loud sounds and comforted by mother's voice.
He can hold his head up briefly while lying on his stomach.
If supported, the infant can sit.
He will follow brightly colored objects.
He is quieted when picked up.
Sucking motions need to be satisfied.
Solid foods are introduced.
He will be sleeping 4-10 hours at night and naps often.
The infant smiles often.
He cries because he is in pain, hungry or uncomfortable.
He makes cooing sounds.

Four to eight months—

The baby can roll from side to side and he can sit alone.
He plays with his hands and can grasp an article.
There are some hand-to-mouth motions at feedings.
He sleeps 10-12 hours with 2 or 3 naps.
He can amuse himself for short intervals.
The baby likes small toys and mirrors.
He is able to tell strangers from parents.
He can respond to his name or the ringing of the telephone.
The baby understands "no-no" and "bye-bye."

Nine to twelve months—

Creeping and crawling is established.
He can pull himself to a standing position and may stand alone.
The baby can put marks on paper as finger-thumb grasp is developed.
Holding his own bottle and drinking from a cup is common.
He can feed himseelf with his fingers and he can hold a spoon.
The baby sleeps 14-16 hours and naps 1 or 2 times.
He is able to put objects together or in or out of containers.
Games like peek-a-boo or pat-a-cake are favorites.
He says "da-da," "ma-ma" and imitates sounds.
He can point to or look at familiar objects or people and wave bye-bye
    when asked.
Simple directions can be followed.
Distraction, substitution and removal are the most effective methods of
    discipline at this age.

AGES AND STAGES

Development of the Pre-Schooler

One to two years—

The child can creep, climb, walk and run.

He needs limits set, and also outlets for his boundless energy.

He likes to throw, dump and fill

The child can speak and respond to a few words and phrases and asks for things by vocalizing and pointing.

Physically, some rudiments of toilet training appear.

A bottle may be given up and a cup held.

He may begin to feed himself and awkwardly extend an arm or leg for dressing.

Socially he treats other children and adults as objects and has no concept of sharing.

His moods are shifting and his temper short-lived.

Removing him bodily from incidents and distraction are best discipline procedures at this age.

Two to three years—

The child is rapidly losing proportions of babyhood.

He speaks in two and three word sentences.

This is the "no-no" stage and "no" is emphatically expressed to all suggestions.

He responds best to routine.

Toilet training is quickly learned.

He is capable of relaxing and feeding himself with some spilling.

His attention span is short, and he needs to move from one activity to another.

Socially his play is mostly solitary (alone) and parallel (plays along with other children, not with them).

He treats children as objects.

He is very possessive and many disputes are a result of this.

The two year-old likes to scribble, making lines, dots and circles.

He enjoys music and can learn simple songs.

Humor or distraction are best approaches to discipline at this age.

Three year-old—

He is developing good motor control.

The baby look is disappearing as arms and legs lengthen.

Physically he can undress, but still needs help dressing.

He manages himself well in all routines, being less rigid and ritualistic.

Socially he begins group play with one or two children, but still enjoys
    playing alone.

He is beginning to share.

He is curious and highly imaginative.

He is more cooperative, more comforming, more eager to please, and is
    getting more interested in people and things about him.

Four year-old—

He is usually very active and assertive with much "out of bounds" behav-
    ior.

He has good motor control.

Four and five word sentences are common. He likes to ramble on and on.

He is very sociable and likes to use exaggeration.

He is often bossy, boastful, indulges in name calling, tattling and argues
    frequently.

The four year old can cooperate with other children in play activities and
    likes to share experiences.

Sexually he is developing friendships with children of his own sex and is
    becoming attached to the opposite sexed parent.

He wants to learn about his body and where he came from.

He is interested in life beyond home and school and reproduces this in his
    play.

Rhythm is developed and he enjoys music.

He can build elaborate block structures and talks about them.

His attention span is longer now.

He is imaginative, dramatic and versatile, constantly asking why and how.

Five year-old—

He has mastered large muscle control but still has difficulty with small muscle control, such as printing.

A difference is recognized between his right and left hand.

He can learn socially accepted behavior and behave in a mannerly way.

He plays well in groups and is cooperative with adults and children.

He likes to listen to stories and learns by imitating.

Questions are many and he wants truthful answers.

The five year-old is more self sufficient and can assume some responsibility such as simple household tasks.

His art work shows representation, a figure becomes himself, or Dad or Mom.

He defines words in terms of use and is more sympathetic and is aware of causes of distress.

Some reasoning can be used with pre-schoolers as a discipline approach.

AGES AND STAGES

Development of the Primary School Aged Child

Six year-old—

He is usually in first grade at school and constantly active whether sitting or standing.

He is still having difficulty coordinating eye and hand movement.

The child is beginning to distinguish between fact and fantasy.

He is noisy and boisterous and inconsistent.

At this age, he is easily excited and violently emotional, loves one minute and hates the next.

He is demanding of others and negative in response, expecting others to conform to his way of thinking and doing.

Because he is self-centered and demanding, he is not able to cooperate too well in organized games.

He seeks approval and does not accept criticism, blame or punishment very well.

It is difficult for him to make decisions or choices.

Lots of praise for accepted behavior works well as discipline at this age.

Seven year-old—

This is an age of frustration.

The child expects too much of himself and wants to do everything perfectly.

This is a more withdrawn age.

He tends to feel that peers, parents and teachers are unfair.

He feels a need for a place in the family and tends to be jealous of siblings.

He complains often and cries frequently.

He likes to be alone and has a "nobody loves me" attitude.

At this age, reading, observing and watching take up a great deal of time.

He is busy touching, feeling and explaining.

He responds best to indirect correction because he tends to worry.

Eight year-old—

Carelessness begins to show.

He often works or plays to the point of exhaustion.

At eight he wants to meet the community.

He prefers to work and play in groups. This is the gang and club stage.

He is interested in relationships with others.

There is an interest in the family group, but he has difficulty getting along with siblings as he is very sensitive.

The eight year-old tries to express his ideas and to take part in activities which are beyond his capacity.

Lots of frustration and angry feelings are expressed.

He is beginning to develop some understanding of space and time.

He responds well to praise and comments on improvement as a discipline method.

AGES AND STAGES

Development of the Pre-Adolescent

Nine, ten and eleven year-old—

This is a period of transition.

Childish patterns of behavior are being discarded. He is developing his own attitudes, independent of adults.

Conduct is inconsistent and disorganized.

He is restless, sensitive and moody.

Signs of sexual development can be seen.

There can be regression to infantile habits of nailbiting, tears, etc.

This is the age of peer or gang influence.

There is strong motivation in group competition and lots of teamwork cooperation. He works well on group projects and enjoys boy-girl competition.

Loyalty to group and family is noticeable.

He is a hero worshipper and is drawn to heroes of his sex and time in all areas.

He has a longer attention span now and increased memory detail.

Details are more clearly seen than main ideas.
He is interested in the concrete and real more than the abstract.
There is an increased mastery of "tool skill," especially reading.
He is a collector and an excellent model builder.
Clear limits are needed on behavior at this time. He needs to know what is
    expected of him and what the consequences will be for his actions.

AGES AND STAGES

Development of the Early Adolescent

Twelve and thirteen year-old—

This is a period of rapid growth, physically, mentally, emotionally and
    socially.
Girls are about two years ahead of boys.
The early adolescent is acutely sensitive about being different.
He develops deep, close relationships with the same sex.
He is acquiring the ability to reason and begins to question authority, no
    longer being content with being told what to do.
He is antagonistic and negative to most adult authority.
The early adolescent wants to know why and can handle abstract con-
    cepts.
He is experiencing the awakening of sexual awareness.
He is searching for the self-image. Who am I? Adult or child? Different
    roles will be acted out in each.
Security and deep love are needed in spite of his being unable to respond.
The standard of peers is more important than the adult world.
He conforms to fads for security.
This age brings a new sense of history and chronology.
There is a strong sense of social justice and he wants to feel needed and
    useful to society.
Being impartial, just and patient will help him to explore and to discover
    his role in life.

AGES AND STAGES

Development of the Adolescent

Fourteen to Adult—

Heterosexual interests need to be developed. There should be normal interest in members of the opposite sex, leading to selection of one mate.

Social maturity consists of having feelings of acceptance by peers, social tolerance and freedom from imitation. He will move from having many friends of the same sex to a solid few. This is the beginning of emancipation, growth of self-control and reliance on self for security, so vital for adulthood.

An interest in a practical occupation, leading to a choice of one, needs to be developed. Goals include a reasonably accurate estimate of the adolescent's own abilities and interests. Active participation in sports, hobbies and clubs will help to fill leisure time now and as an adult.

A philosophy of life needs to develop. The adolescent must learn to identify with possible goals, rather than impossible goals. He needs to form his own value system. Lots of testing will occur in the process.

Intellectual maturity requires evidence before acceptance of truth on the basis of authority. He needs a desire for the explanation of facts. His many temporary interests need to turn toward a few stable ones.

Emotionally he needs to learn to handle his feelings. He needs to know feelings are not negative or positive in themselves but that he will be held accountable for the actions of his feelings.

Physically his body is changing into an adult. Although he has the basic facts of life at this age, he needs answers to his abstract questions on sex, such as what is love and an explanation of his moodiness.

GROWTH STAGES THROUGH THE MEDIA OF ART

Art is a media that visually demonstrates how children grow in ages and stages. All children progress through these stages if they are not "kept back." Viktor Lowenfeld in his book *Creative and Mental Growth* mentions the following stages of development in art work.

1. Scribbling Stage, children 2 to 4 years of age

   - There are 17 basic patterns of scribbling
   - First stage of scribbling is implied, no pattern
   - Second stage consists of outlines, circles, ovals and squares
   - Placement on paper varies from a small area to covering the whole page

2. Early Pictoral and Representational Stage, 4 to 7 years of age

   - Use of mandolas or suns with radials
   - Rough forms of objects, people, trees, and animals
   - Radials are extended from the circle called the sun to make a semblance of a human form
   - Size of object usually is determined by the importance to the child

3. Achieving Form Concept, 7 to 9 years of age

   - More detail is given to figures
   - A sky line and base or ground line is added
   - Figures eventually will set on the base line

4. Children Are Aware of Realism, 9 to 11 years of age

- Children try to visualize reality
- Children's drawings will overlap, one building over another or a boy in front of a fence
- Drawings are flat with no depth perspective
- Sky line and base line meet
- Repetition of objects is evident

5. Stage of Reasoning, 11 to 13 years of age

- Use of color and proportion
- Experimentation with materials
- Use of action in drawings

6. Making Decisions, adolescence

- Time of critical awareness of the environment
- Lights and shadows are expressed
- Three dimensional qualities are used
- Value relationships of objects can be seen

●Remember it takes professionals to analyze children's art work but you can observe your child's work and notice the similarities in the above stages. Never assume what your child has drawn. Ask him to tell you about it.

OBSERVING GROWTH PATTERNS OF YOUR PRE-SCHOOL AGED CHILD

1. What word or words best describe your child?

    _____happy   _____cautious

    _____joyous   _____bubbly

    _____fearful   _____unhappy

    _____angry   _____withdrawn

2. How does your child relate to his peers?

3. Does he seek attention from children and adults by saying "Look at me," "I know how," or "Let me do that"?

4. Does he follow directions easily?

5. How does he handle his emotions?

    _____crying

    _____temper tantrums

    _____physical fighting

    _____other

6. What are his favorite play materials?

7. How does he relate to adults other than you?

8. What characteristics is he developing that will be valuable to him as an adult?

OBSERVING GROWTH PATTERNS OF YOUR ELEMENTARY SCHOOL AGED CHILD

1. Is he developing physically appropriate to his age and body frame?

2. Does he have trouble with reading skills?

3. Do you notice signs of abstract thinking?

4. What word or words best describe your child?

_____"out of bounds"   _____sensitive

_____considerate   _____secretive

_____passive   _____uncooperative

_____lovable   _____bossy

_____moody   _____other

5. Has he begun to develop sexually?

6. Is it difficult for him to concentrate?

7. How does your child feel about himself?

_____confident

_____unsure

8. Does he communicate freely?

9. Has he learned to share and take turns?

10. Can he make friends easily?

11. Does he relate to adults as well as peers?

12. Can he handle responsibility along with privileges?

OBSERVING GROWTH PATTERNS OF YOUR PREADOLESCENT AND ADOLESCENT CHILD

Communication

1. Does he enjoy conversations with you?
2. Is he willing, anxious, or reluctant to talk?
3. Does he pay close attention to what you say?
4. Does he accept what you say or does he seem to be trying to judge for himself?
5. Can he express himself?

Physical Maturity

1. Has he begun to develop sexually?
2. Have menstruation or wet dreams begun?
3. How does he handle his awkwardness as his body grows at such a rapid rate?
4. Do you notice a draining of energy often mistaken for laziness during this growth period?

Mental Maturity

1. How does he handle abstract ideas?
2. Does he think things out or make snap judgments?
3. Can he follow directions?
4. How does he feel about school and learning?
5. Does he have an adequate attention span?
6. Does he have a hobby or interest?

Emotional Maturity

1. Is he happy in a school environment?
2. Does he bite his nails or show other signs of pressure?
3. Does he fluctuate between being adult and child?
4. Is he moody?
5. Is he shy or outgoing?
6. Is he sensitive to others' needs?
7. How does he feel about himself?

Social Maturity

1. Does he question authority?
2. Whose standards are more important to him, those of his friends or of adults?
3. Has he established heterosexual relationships?
4. Does he have a sense of social justice?
5. What kinds of physical activity does he like?
6. What kinds of TV programs does he watch?
7. How does he spend his leisure time?
8. Has he begun to prepare for an occupation?

"YOUR CHILDREN ARE NOT YOUR CHILDREN.
THEY ARE THE SONS AND DAUGHTERS OF LIFE'S LONGING FOR
   ITSELF.
THEY COME THROUGH YOU BUT NOT FROM YOU.
AND THOUGH THEY ARE WITH YOU, YET THEY BELONG NOT TO
   YOU.
YOU MAY GIVE THEM YOUR LOVE BUT NOT YOUR THOUGHTS,
FOR THEY HAVE THEIR OWN THOUGHTS.
YOU MAY HOUSE THEIR BODIES, BUT NOT THEIR SOULS,
FOR THEIR SOULS DWELL IN THE HOUSE OF TOMORROW,
   WHICH YOU CANNOT VISIT, NOT EVEN IN YOUR DREAMS.
YOU MAY STRIVE TO BE LIKE THEM, BUT SEEK NOT TO
   MAKE THEM LIKE YOU.
FOR LIFE GOES NOT BACKWARD NOR TARRIES WITH
   YESTERDAY.
YOU ARE THE BOWS FROM WHICH YOUR CHILDREN
   AS LIVING ARROWS ARE SENT FORTH."

Kahlil Gibran, **The Prophet**

NOTES

*If we were ever to be
able to raise a butterfly,
we must care for
a caterpillar*

DISCIPLINE, MEANING & ALTERNATIVES

DISCIPLINE

"Parenthood is an endless series of small events, periodic conflicts, and sudden crises, which call for a response . . . Love is not enough. Insight is insufficient. Good parents need skill."
Dr. Haim Ginott, **Between Parent and Teenager**

So much has been written on the terrible trials of discipline. The joy has been left out. Discipline can be a joyous goal to accomplish. First we must determine what we mean by discipline. Discipline is a considered plan for teaching a child how to live usefully and happily with himself and with others. There is not only one plan that accomplishes successful discipline, it's the combination of positive alternatives that is most workable. Whatever plan is used it must be a plan that is thought out. Discipline must teach. If the form of discipline that you use does not teach, then it is not discipline. What do we want to teach our child? We want him to be able to live usefully, to feel a sense of accomplishment to himself and to the world he will live in. We want him to do this happily. He needs to think well of himself. If he is happy with himself and with others, he will experience true success.

Why do we discipline children? Safety is needed to protect our lives. We want our children to wear seat belts, proper clothes for play, take precautions in recreation and in our homes. It takes discipline to submit to safety features in our daily lives.

We are health conscious today more than ever before. Discipline is needed to eat the proper foods, see the doctor or dentist, and work with environmentalists for clean air and water. Life is a precious gift from God and we want to protect it.

Children interact with other children and adults. It is nice to be around children who show common courtesies to make life more pleasant. Knowing courtesies is not inherited. "Thank you" and "please" must be learned.

Discipline is needed for order in our lives. Look around you. All the world was created to work orderly. Our bodies are a perfect example of order and harmony. We have more time for ourselves if we arrange our day in an orderly way.

Disciplined children and parents give all family members peace of mind. We need peace of mind to function effectively.

In general, to learn is to be disciplined. Our minds are constantly searching for truth. We were created that way.

Sexuality is one area where discipline is needed. Your teenager needs to know that his sexual feelings are a part of him and beautiful, but that he is responsible for his relationship with another person. It takes discipline to see sex and love wedded together.

Ultimately the most important goal of discipline is to be self-disciplined. Our children need to learn to think for themselves and make decisions accordingly. The alternatives to discipline we will be discussing will help our children to become self-disciplined.

Let's look at some present day concepts of child rearing. Parental authority needs to come from love and trust. History shows us that this is a fairly new concept. A child's life prior to modern times was unbearable. Physical abuse and the use of children for personal gratification was a matter of fact. Children are not evil of themselves nor are they miniature adults. These were concepts generally accepted. Children want to please their parents and respond to their parents' belief in them.

Parents have a moral obligation to guide their child to a free and responsible obedience based on understanding and insight. We definitely have an advantage over our children physically and intellectually. This gives us power. We must be careful how we use this power if we are to develop a long lasting, loving relationship with our child. Authoritative power only lasts as long as the child is dependent on us. If love and trust have not been developed, the relationship based on power alone will die.

Parent-child relationships are more important than what rules, rewards, or punishments you use as long as no extremes of punishment or permissiveness are used and as long as your approach is fairly consistent. Look for signs of the relationship you have with your child. You will know that you have a positive relationship with your child if he comes and hugs or touches you, if he wants to talk and be with you, if occasionally he helps when he isn't asked, and if he tells his feelings to you. If you find you are frequently angry with your child, or that small problems become an issue; or that you find yourself name calling and yelling or hitting your child, these might be signs of a poor relationship.

There needs to be a positive atmosphere in the family to develop initiative and freedom. There should not be a smothering with commands. On a piece of paper write down the number of times you say "no" to your child in a day. Are all the "no's" really thought out? Could you have worded your response positively? Such as "You need to come to dinner now," rather than "No, you can't play now." Nagging reinforces the very behavior we do not want by calling attention to that behavior. To avoid nagging, be sure the child is listening. Your presence, eye contact, and body language will assure you the child is listening. Use a vocabulary that is suitable for the age of the child you are talking to. Directions need to be stated in a positive way. For instance "It's time to come to dinner," not, "Would you please come to dinner?" The second statement gives the child a chance to say an emphatic "No." Give a series of directions one at a time or in order of expected performance according to age and ability. A four year-old can handle one or two directions given at a time, a twelve year-old, three or four. Adults have trouble with more than four directions at a given time.

Parents need to help children grow toward greater independence by giving the minimum of help even though there is the risk of errors and mistakes. We are raising our children to leave us. They need to be independent. It is easier to do the job ourselves, to make the beds the right way or to wash the dishes and make sure they are clean, but remember we are teaching. He needs to learn to do it himself. Show him the way but give him the opportunity to learn to do it himself. A two year-old can carry a small waste basket to empty, a ten year-old can cut the grass, and a sixteen year-old can handle a chain saw if taught properly. When a mistake is made, such as carrying a glass of milk and spilling the contents, the mess needs to be cleaned up. Simple comments as "Let me show you an easier way. You'll need to clean up the mess. Here's a sponge." teach the child mistakes are made but he can try again without losing his self-image.

You need to learn the underlying causes of your child's behavior. Why did he do what he has done? There could be physical reasons, not enough sleep, not feeling well, not able to see or hear adequately, etc. Jealousy could be a problem with his brothers and sisters. There could be a problem at school with teachers or his peer group. It is important that you watch his body language and listen to your child's words. He is telling you so much.

Let the child know you understand how he feels and that you have felt that way at times. He needs to know he is not the only one that can hate and love interchangeably. Emotions are positive in themselves. There are no negative or positive feelings. All feelings make up who we are. It's the expression of these feelings that are positive or negative and that make us accountable. Your child needs to learn that he cannot physically hurt someone with his angry feelings, but he can get some wood and nails and begin pounding. It is important to give children alternatives that are acceptable to you in expressing their feelings. He cannot kick the dog when he is angry but he can punch his pillow. Children need to know that you also have a right to your feelings. Tell your child how you are feeling and why. This will open discussion on what can be done to help family members feel better.

Children need lots of encouragement and praise to achieve acceptable behavior. Remember, behavior is learned. Praises like, "I like the way you tried," feel good when your child fails at something. You might want to add "Let me show you an easier way to do it." A smile, a hug, both will encourage your child to try again. A reward once-in-awhile, such as lunch out with Dad is a great incentive to keep trying.

There are preventions we can use in avoiding discipline problems. "An ounce of prevention is worth a pound of cure." Accept your child for who he is. He is a unique individual and different from any other child in the world.

Develop obedience by reason not fear. A child needs, and can accept, an explanation according to his age and ability of why he may or may not do something. For example, "You may not jump on the couch because you might hurt yourself or damage my new couch. Use your jumping board in the yard." A child, no matter how young, is entitled to a reason. For a young child, express the reason simply. In the above example notice an alternative is provided. This lets the child know what he can do that is acceptable to you. Instilling fear in a child may temporarily cease a discipline problem but can cause problems later in adulthood. Such as "If you hit your brother, God will punish you." What happens when he falls and scraps his knee or he isn't chosen for the football team? God will be blamed. Or, "If you don't take your medicine, I'll take you to the doctor for a shot." What happens when he has to have a shot? Hysteria. "See that policeman on the corner, if you don't sit down, he'll put you in jail." The child learns to avoid policemen at all costs. Then to confuse the issue we tell him to call a policeman for help if he is lost. If he won't sit in the car, pull over and stop until he does. This is teaching him what will happen if he cannot follow a safety rule.

Give the child a choice only when you mean to offer a choice. Help him make a decision on choices you approve. "Would you like a fruit, cookies and milk, or cereal for a snack?" Any one he chooses would be acceptable to you. If there is no choice, then make your statement positive. Try "It is time for dinner. You need to come in and wash." Not, "Would you like to come in for dinner?" Be ready to accept "no" for an answer. Decision making takes training. Children need to recognize that there are differences between being able to make a choice and situations where there are no choices.

Let the child have experiences. This will help him to relate to the world around him. A simple walk around the block to observe construction, plants, or animals is very meaningful. The community offers many available opportunities for experiences such as festivals, parades, libraries, government buildings, police and fire stations, etc. Collecting objects for hobbies, a pet, building projects, or travel, all provide experiences and help a child to develop creativeness. Creativeness will help your child to develop uniquely.

Avoid comparing one child with another. Comparisons, positive or negative, are dangerous because they lead to feelings of resentment, jealousy, and insecurity. There is enough competition in the world without promoting this in the family. Support is a more constructive way of motivating behavior. For instance "If you finish cleaning your room, we'll have time to go shopping." Or "I'll help you with this problem you're having trouble with." So much better than, "Why can't you keep your room like your sister?" Or "Boy, are you dumb! Your brother never had trouble with his arithmetic."

Redirecting a child's activity will prevent a behavior problem. It is best to choose an activity which coincides with his interests. "Bobby, that record playing will wake your sister from her nap. Yesterday, Betty called and asked for you to help her repair her bike. This would be a good time." Learn how to forestall and prevent trouble by proper timing. Offer a supporting hand before a child falls, arbitrate before two children begin a first fight, suggest a new activity before the group grows restless, and change the location of ball throwing before the window is broken. Re-direction requires imagination, time, and thought but the results make parenting a joy.

Communication is an important tool to use with your child in preventing discipline problems. Talk to your teenager on an adult level. Let him in on the decision making and planning of the family. Set aside a time at least once a week when the family can be open and discuss feelings, problems, chores, rules, and future plans. Each member needs an opportunity to talk without interruption. This is an important way of building a trust relationship, the "give and take" so vital in family living.

Replace physical punishment with other methods of discipline. Physical punishment teaches children that it is permissable to hit to solve a problem. No one feels good after being hit or hitting. Many times it is a release for our feelings but teaches nothing. As parents we need to channel our feelings into acceptable outlets before disciplining our children. At times we all give in to this method, but there are alternative approaches that are more effective. As parents we are told that spankings should be avoided but we are not told what to do. What are other alternative solutions to spankings?

The very young child needs love and care. He really is not misbehaving to get even with you. The best way to teach him what is acceptable to you is to distract him, or remove him or the object he is after and substitute an acceptable object. Slapping a toddler may stop the action but often times does not. Or, it is stopped only because you are around and then he becomes very frustrated and may feel not wanted by you. Hitting gives the unmistakable message "I'm not worth very much."

The reward system can be very effective in changing a behavior pattern for all ages of children. As adults we use this method often. Your pay check is a reinforcer for the work you do. After losing weight, a new outfit reinforces you to keep that new weight. By using reinforcers, an unacceptable behavior pattern can be changed to an acceptable one. It is important that only one problem is handled at a time. Reinforcers can be social or non-social. Social reinforcers are words and gestures we use to show pleasure or approval. "I'm so proud of you. You did a fine job." A hug or kiss or pat on the back are social reinforcers. These need to be given for acceptable behavior. The more we call attention to unacceptable behavior by shouting and raving, the more that behavior will continue especially if the child is craving attention. More than likely the child learns how to "turn you off."

Non-social reinforcers can be concrete rewards such as points or stars that can then be accumulated to purchase a wanted item. Money or certain foods can be used. Behaviorists show amazing results in achieving acceptable behavior. The trick is to know how and when to ease up on non-social reinforcers. As behavior improves, the reward is given every other time, then once a week, and finally taken away completely and substituted with a social reinforcer.

Activities such as games, a week-end fishing trip, a visit to the zoo are also reinforcers. You need to know what your child likes to do. Decide on the reinforcer together. Reinforcers give a child incentive to work for a behavior change that will be acceptable to you.

A time-out is effective with young children. Removing a child from a problem situation and putting him in a room for a short period of time gives him a chance to evaluate the situation. The choice is his. He either choses to change the behavior pattern or he goes into a time-out. He always needs a chance to try again.

Privileges and responsibilities provide another alternative for discipline. This works especially well with older children. We seldom talk to our children about the privileges of being in a family. It is important to do so. The child can see the value of responsibility in the family. With privileges there are responsibilities that can be decided by the child and parent. When a responsibility is not achieved, then the privilege is taken away. For example, "I'm sorry you won't be able to have the car next week-end. Driving the car is a privilege and you helped make the rule about curfew and calling home if detained. You come in late. The decision was yours." It is even better to have your responsibilities and rules written down. This takes you "off the hook" when the child claims he can't remember. The child learns to make a decision by himself and face the consequences of that decision.

Use consequences when ever possible. This is how learning takes place. "Since you are not brushing your teeth regularly, you may have no sweets. When you begin brushing your teeth regularly, you may have desserts again." (Notice you always give the child a chance to try again.) Or, "I'm sorry you may not eat now. We had our meal and you chose not to eat. Breakfast will be served in the morning." The feeling of hunger is a natural consequence of not eating. A missed meal will not damage your child, and the lesson learned is invaluable.

Some consequences occur naturally as a result of an action. Other consequences need to be improvised. We would not allow a child to get hit by a car if he runs in the street (natural consequence) so we need to restrict him to the house or yard and try again later.

In disciplining your older child, a "no win-no lose" approach works best. You should not "win" over your child, nor should he feel he has "won" over you. A compromising effort will bring joy in parenting. Respect the child as an individual with dignity.

Be careful not to use money as punishment. Our children need to learn how to handle money if they are to function as an adult in our "money world." This is an area of parenting that is neglected. Sit down and plan a budget with your child. A child entering school is not too young to begin to learn to handle money. Decide what expenses he and you will be responsible for. Set the amount of money together, being careful to allow a little extra that the child can spend exactly as he wants—perhaps to save for something special or to spend on a whim. No matter, it is his decision. Do not pay children for chores that contribute to the family well-being. Those need to be divided among all family members. If the child wishes to earn more money you might give him the opportunity to do a chore over and above the usual. By taking away money for punishment, you may find yourself in a bind when his allowance is all gone. What do you take away then? Use one of the alternatives we discussed to solve a discipline problem.

These alternative methods to hitting and yelling help the child to learn self-discipline, the ultimate goal of disciplining. We cannot always be around our children. They need to make decisions for themselves. Hitting does not fulfill this goal. Discipline that does not lower self-image is possible. Remember, the discipline skills you are using with your child will be what he will use someday as a parent. Parents tend to parent as they have been parented, unless they have been exposed to alternatives.

Although the above methods all require more time and effort, the outcome is rewarding and successful as your child matures into adulthood. He will feel good about himself and others and this will bring joy to you as a parent.

DISCIPLINE

1. How did your parents discipline you as a child?

2. Did your mother and father differ in their methods of discipline? Did they agree?

3. Did you learn how to play-off one against the other?

4. Were your parents consistent?

5. Did one of your parents always say "ask your mother" or "ask your father" when faced with a decision regarding you?

6. What are your early recollections of discipline in school?

7. At the time, did you feel the discipline you received was generally fair?

8. What feelings do you have when you discipline a child?

EFFECTIVE CONCEPTS IN DISCIPLINE

Discipline is a considered plan for teaching a child how to live usefully and happily with himself and with others.

1. Our guidance as parents needs to be based on trust and love. Authority can become power, and power must not be used to break a child's will.

2. Children need to be guided to learning self-discipline in preparation for emancipation. This is the ultimate goal of discipline.

3. From the time your child was born, you should be raising him to leave you.

4. Relationships are an important factor in discipline. Develop a positive relationship with your child.

5. Give your child responsibility even though he may make mistakes. We learn by our mistakes. Give him that opportunity to learn.

6. Children need to know the privileges of family living in order to accept the responsibilities.

7. The timing of a suggestion is as important as the suggestion itself. Effective discipline depends on knowing how to prevent trouble by proper timing. Suggest a better place to play before the ball goes into the street.

8. Help your child accept his feelings and learn how to channel them into proper outlets, outlets that are acceptable to you. (See the chapter on Emotions and Feelings.)

9. Be sure your child knows that you understand how he feels because you have the same feelings. He will learn how to handle his feelings by watching you handle yours.

10. Parents need to feel good about themselves so that they can feel good about and enjoy their children.

PREVENTING DISCIPLINE PROBLEMS

1. Listen and observe your child. Skill in listening and observing is helpful in building our understanding of children's behavior.

2. Help the child develop his individuality. Do not stifle his learning with a smothering of "no's" and commands.

3. Accept differences among children. Avoid encouraging competition or making comparisons between children.

4. Understand the concepts your child is capable of at his age level.

5. Develop obedience in children by reason, not fear.

6. State suggestions or directions in a positive way. If there is no response, follow with a positive discipline action. This will help to avoid power struggles.

7. Give a child a few minutes before changing activity.

8. Make your suggestions effective by your body presence. Yelling from another room is not effective.

9. Use words to build the child's self-image instead of blaming, shaming, or making him feel guilty.

10. State a command when you do not want your child to have a choice. "It's time for dinner." If there is a choice, state a request, "Would you like dessert now?"

11. Let the child have experiences.

12. Set aside a time at least once a week when the family can meet to discuss feelings, problems, chores, rules, and future plans. Every member needs a chance to talk without interruption or punishment. Compromise whenever possible.

DISCIPLINE

Buzz Questions

1. How do children misbehave?

2. Why do children misbehave?

3. Why is it so difficult to discipline children?

4. How do children learn to behave?

5. How can we as parents gain their cooperation?

DISCIPLINE

Try these alternatives to spanking, yelling and nagging your children. Spanking may stop an action temporarily, but hitting lowers self-image and teaches children to solve their problems by hitting. The following methods will stop the action, teach your child acceptable behavior and will not lower self-image.

1. The best discipline for children under three is removal or distraction and substitution. Your child learns by touching. When he goes after that prize vase, remove it and give him something else to hold. Hitting him is not more effective than removing him. Removing him and giving him something else is teaching him what he may not do, and what he may do. Praise him when he pleases you. Do not give him attention for unacceptable behavior.

2. **Reinforcers.** This method is successful for all ages of children. Reinforce your child's positive behavior by social reinforcers (hug, kiss, words of praise, smile) or non-social reinforcers (gold stars on a chart, lunch with you, trip to the zoo, ice cream). Pick only one behavior pattern you want to correct. Explain to your child your feelings and what you want to do to help him change that behavior. Make a chart and agree on a reinforcer. Set the time-limit according to the age of the child. A one day time-limit may be a real accomplishment if the behavior problem is happening often. With younger children the reinforcers may have to be changed before the goal is accomplished. When the behavior is corrected, return to a social reinforcer.

3. **Time-out.** This method works best from three to ten years of age. Choose one behavior pattern you want to correct. Explain to your child your feelings and what you are going to do to help him correct his behavior. Pick a room (a chair in a corner will do) that will not provide entertainment. The bathroom is usually suggested. Be sure to remove breakables. Get a timer and explain to the child when he is misbehaving (specify problem) he will go into the room for a certain length of time. One to fifteen minutes is all the time that is needed to learn. Set the timer and begin when the child is quiet in the room. Be consistent each time the behavior occurs. For a young child you may need to stand by the door. Praise the child as the behavior is corrected, but say nothing when it is not. Just put him in time-out.

4. **Natural and logical consequences.** This method is effective for all ages of children. For every act we do there is a consequence, and we learn by our consequences. A natural consequence is one that follows an act naturally. If your child forgets his lunch, he will go hungry. A logical consequence is one made up when a natural one cannot be allowed. When your child runs into the street, you cannot let him get hit by a car. An effective, logical consequence is to place him in a confined area to play until he learns he may not go into the street. Be sure the consequence is as close to the act as possible for best results. This discipline procedure teaches the child to become responsible for his own actions. Forgetting his lunch becomes his problem, not yours. Being put in a confined area is his choice, not yours.

5. **Privileges and responsibilities.** This approach is most effective with older children. Discuss the privileges you share together in a family companionship; love, food, shelter, etc. Then discuss responsibilities each member has to assume to make your family run smoothly. Write them down so your children can refer to them often. Make chores more fun by rotating them. No one likes to empty garbage for 10 years. When responsibilities are not met, privileges are taken away. Do not make the removal of the privilege unreasonable. One night, or weekend, is enough. The learning is happening. If a room is not cleaned, then a friend cannot come over. Be careful about taking allowances away for lack of responsibility. Use allowances to teach your child how to manage money. Do not pay your child for responsibilities he does at home. However, he may choose to do a job over and above his normal duties to earn extra spending money.

6. **Use compromise whenever possible.** There does not have to be a winner or a loser in disciplining. Set limits together as a family. This is especially important with your older children. Because of peer pressure, if your child wants to wear his hair longer, fine; but he must keep it neat and clean.

7. **Communication.** This is effective for all ages of children. The way we talk to our children can prevent or lead to discipline problems. (See sheet on communication that develops positive self-image). Listening effectively and talking positively encourage positive behavior. Not giving choices causes a child to rebel. Labeling puts a child on defense. An "I feel" response is more effective than a "you make me" response.

Remember, spanking, yelling, nagging all reinforce the negative behavior you want to change. When you discipline be sure you state what he may not do, a simple reason why not, and then what he may do.

HOW TO FEEL GOOD ABOUT DISCIPLINING

Watch for behavior that is acceptable to you. Then praise your child with words and body language for what he has done. The more often you show your children what is acceptable to you, the more they will respond with good behavior. Praising your children will show them you are pleased with their behavior and they will want to repeat this behavior.

No child is born into the world sociably acceptable. This is learned. Here are some skills for you to work with to teach your child acceptable behavior.

1. Work on one problem at a time. You can't change all behavior overnight.

2. Try to understand why your child is behaving the way he is. Was the child up late last night? Did he lose a friend?

3. Decide what you can do to help the situation. Should the child rest now? Should you take the time now to be a friend and listen to your child?

4. Help your child improve his behavior by giving reinforcements. A smile, a hug, or a touch tells a child his behavior is improving.

5. Let your child be responsible for the consequences of his acts. If your child loses his baseball mitt, let him do extra chores to help earn money for a new one.

6. Avoid hitting your children. Hitting teaches violence and to solve problems by hitting. If you handle your feelings first, most likely you will not need to hit. No one feels good after hitting or being hit.

7. Yelling and nagging reinforce negative behavior. The most effective speech is simple, direct, slow and quiet.

8. Be consistent in using positive discipline.

9. Communicate with your child. Listen and be non-judgmental. Allow him to try to come to his own decisions. Let your child know you are there to help. Listen to his feelings and tell him yours.

10. Decide on rules and limits together. The older the child, the more he needs a voice in setting limits. Write your agreements down. This will take you "off the hook" when your child says, "I don't remember that we said that."

OBSERVATION ON DISCIPLINE

REMEMBER—Discipline is a considered plan for teaching a child how to live usefully and happily with himself and with others.

1. List what your child does that pleases you as you observe him during the week.

2. List what your child does that bothers you.

3. During the week observe occasions when you discipline your child (perhaps positively or negatively). Briefly give an example of each occasion.

4. Watch for and record two or three examples of what you consider "good discipline" by another parent.

a. How did the child react?

b. What did you like about the way the person handled it?

5. Children learn self-discipline (self-control) and to accept limits. Give examples of your child's disciplined behavior.

DISCIPLINE

D — is for distraction, the best device a parent can use to divert a child's attention away from undesirable actions to more acceptable behavior.

I — is for independence, a trait most children possess and one that should be directed, not destroyed.

S — is for security, something all children need and want.

C — is for consistency, a quality parents should strive for in guiding children in order to help them achieve security.

I — is for insist, something all parents must do at times. Parents who have firm convictions on what they regard as acceptable behavior and who refuse to give way to outside pressures are likely to have better-adjusted children.

P — is for praise, which should be given freely when a child deserves it.

L — is for love, the key word to the whole problem of behavior. Each child needs to love and to be loved.

I — is for individual, and each child is one in his own right. Each child has certain inborn personality traints and should be loved and accepted for himself.

N — is for negatives; the "no, stop, don't" words which are often overworked in handling children. Negative words should be used only when necessary in order to maintain their effectiveness.

E — is for example, and each parent should set a good one. The child is more likely to do what he sees done rather than what he is told to do.

Put them all together and you spell DISCIPLINE, a subject that is of much concern to all parents.

Source Unknown

NOTES

To love someone is to give them room enough to grow

SIBLING RIVALRY, INTERACTIONS BETWEEN SIBLINGS

SIBLING RIVALRY

"Lord, make me a channel of thy peace . . . that where there is discord I may bring harmony . . ."

Saint Francis of Assisi

Sibling rivalry is the interaction between brothers and sisters. It is how brothers and sisters get along with each other and all the feelings and emotions involved. By living with brothers and sisters, children learn how to interact with peers. What they learn in the family extends to their social relationships.

Are families normal when brothers and sisters quarrel? Families live in close proximity. There are bound to be disagreements. I would worry about a family that had no disagreements. For, if each member is an individual, as they need to be, then disagreements will happen. Angry feelings usually cover up a hidden feeling. Your child may be very angry with his sister because he was upset when you told him he could not watch tv. Disagreements are normal, but physical or emotional damage to others is not. Children need to be aware that feelings are part of us, but we are responsible for our reactions to them. There are rules when we live in a family. It is all right to be angry, but we cannot hurt ourselves or others. Provide channels for their angry feelings that are acceptable to you. Perhaps a pillow could be punched or some large play equipment outside could be used, or maybe it's time to make playdough so the child can punch dough with all his might.

Why do children quarrel? There may be physical reasons such as an illness coming on, not enough sleep, or the routine changed for one reason or another. A common reason for quarreling is trying to get mom and dad's attention. It usually works. Running into a room to separate children gives the children your undivided attention. Usually, we do not know what has happened. We tend to side with the injured child, causing feelings of resentment among the other children.

Proximity in ages, learning to share, competition, jealousy and just plain frustration can lead to quarreling. Problems in school or with peers may trigger a child to take his frustrations out on his brothers and sisters. Close quarters in a home, boredom, or just being tired of the same people living together can cause quarreling.

One mother who was a single parent come to me for help. She had five boys and all had to sleep in the same room, an attic dormitory. The boys were constantly quarreling. The oldest boy slept near the door and kept his belongings all over the floor in such a way that the others couldn't even get into the room. Mother was tired of screaming and yelling. These boys needed some privacy. I suggested she get some large cardboard dividers. Refrigerator packing boxes work well. She set these up as screens between the beds. The boys could decorate them anyway they wanted to. The oldest boy had a choice, to clean up his area or move to the back of the room. He chose to move back. The quarreling was cut down to 20%.

Children quarrel in endless fashions. Hitting, biting, pinching and other physical manifestations are common among young children. Verbal abuse such as name-calling, tattling and teasing become prominent in the primary ages and continue on into adolescense. Ignoring a brother or sister who is desperately trying to get his point across is a very effective way to quarrel. Taking something of value from an opponent provides satisfaction or revenge. Withdrawal from family members or irritability toward them can be a sign of sibling rivalry.

The position of the child in the family plays an important role in sibling rivalry. The oldest child has had mom and dad alone for a time. He is used to attention. Usually, he is given the most responsibility. He has a strong desire to be first and this can cause rivalry with siblings.

The middle child is born into a different family than his older brother or sister. His family consists of a mother, a father and a child. He never has had mom and dad alone. He is constantly vying for mom and dad's attention and one way is to tease his younger brother or sister. This usually gets mom and dad involved. He tends to be more adventurous than his older brother or sister.

The baby in the family is a manipulator and learns to play his brother and sister off against each other. A loud scream when he is hit, even though he has been the instigator, will bring mother running. Mother has not seen what has happened and so will "love" baby and scold the other children who should "know better." He usually has decisions made for him and is given little responsibility.

The only child grows up among adults. It is difficult for him to learn to share and socialize with children unless he is given the opportunity. His rivalry is acted out in his peer group.

Twins, or other multiple births, are a unique position. Many times identity is lost with one twin, unless the parents work to develop individuality.

Position in a family can change. A new baby will rearrange the family constellation. The previously youngest child now becomes the middle child or the oldest. After remarriage, children from both sets of parents may live together, changing the roles of oldest, middle and youngest in the family. A death of a child or an adopted child will change positions. Every position has advantages and disadvantages. It is important to know what these are so we can be supportive of our children.

Parents often wonder why their children are so different. "I treat my children all alike. I've raised them the same way. Why are they so different?" It is impossible to treat all children exactly alike. First of all, genes are put together differently in children. Inherited tendencies will cause children to react in a different manner. Each of your children was not born into the same family. Your oldest child was born into a family with a mother and father. Your second child was born into a family of a mother, father and another child, and so on.

Age span, as well as the sex of a child, plays a part in sibling rivalry. The closer together in age, usually the more squabbling that takes place. Research shows us however, that these same children are closer to one another after they leave home. Being a girl in the middle position of two brothers will have a different result in interactions than a boy in the middle position between two sisters.

We tend to identify with the child in the position we held in our own family. We can better understand what it means to be the oldest in the family if we were. Perhaps one of your children reminds you of your brother whom you did not get along with. This might influence how you handle the child. If you suspect this, consult with your partner or a friend to see if this is indeed the situation. Have your husband or wife take over with this child until you can put your feelings in perspective. You may not be able to change the positions in your family, but knowing about family constellations will make you more sensitive to your child and you will be better able to guide him through the advantages and disadvantages of his position.

There are many feelings and emotions involved in sibling rivalry. Anger and jealousy are the more obvious emotions. Fear, failure, fairness, revenge, hatred, frustration, resentment are feelings that are experienced. What to do with these feelings can be frightening to a child who loves his family.

Jealousy is a feeling that makes us want to protect what we have. It is a very strong feeling for many children. It won't go away and needs to be brought out into the open and talked about. Jealousy needs to be managed with frankness and honesty. As parents there are preventions we can use to help a jealous child. Do not add fuel to the fire by comparing one child to another. Comparisons cause children to act out rivalry. Praise a child for his individuality. "You are learning to clean your room," rather than, "Your side still isn't as clean as your sister's." Try hard not to give a favorite or easier child more privileges. Some children are easier to rear. Try to be as fair as possible to all your children. It is important to note that our children have personalities that may clash with ours. Perhaps you are a perfectionist and keep your room very clean. Your child does only what he has to do. Conflict may arise. Recognize this. Be realistic about your demands and work harder to get along with this child.

Help a child who is bothered by jealousy to find satisfactions of his own in life. Help him find friends and recreation he can enjoy. A new hobby or interest can make him feel good about himself. If a child feels good about himself, he will be able to handle his jealous feelings.

As parents, we need to keep in mind that we have our own feelings in reaction to our children's quarreling. We may feel totally frustrated, anger may swell up in us and we lash out at the children. We may fear that we are not rearing our children properly; "No one can have the monster that I have." "How can I be fair?" "Must I count out every grain of cereal to be sure each child gets an equal amount?" Feelings of resentment may occur: "Why did I have children?" And, of course, the feeling of failure comes to us all. "Where is the joy in raising children?" "Will I ever regain my self-esteem as a parent?" These feelings happen to all of us.

There are ways that we as parents can lessen children's quarrels so the family can function in a healthy way. Possessions are necessary to develop values in life. Too many possessions, or lack of them, can cause problems. Every child needs a few things that are his very own that do not have to be shared. Help your child to sort his toys by putting some in a box and calling them "share toys." These he can share with his brothers and sisters. The other toys that he does not want to share he needs to put away. Each week these toys can be gone through and some of them will more than likely be changed from share toys to personal toys, or vice versa. A child can only value the possessions and property of others if he values his own. He needs the feeling of ownership and the responsibility that goes along with it.

Space, no matter how small an area, is necessary. A drawer, a corner of a room or a special box will do. It is not possible for every child to have his own room, but steps can be taken to be sure he has his own part of a room. Dividers, separate dressers and beds all help him to have the feeling of his own space.

Privacy is needed by everyone. A time to be alone is vital for self-image. Simple courtesies, such as knocking at the bedroom door before entering, develop respect for privacy. Children need to be taught respect for family members who desire privacy. This is not instinctive; it must be learned. At about 9 years of age, children become very conscious regarding bathroom privacy. Siblings need to respect this and learn that in turn their privacy will be respected.

Every child must feel he is good at something. He can do something as well, or better, than anyone else in his family. One child may be able to bake a delicious cake, while another may bring home good grades; another can build with wood. It is important to remember to recognize this ability. One child is no more important than the other because he brings home good grades. We all excel in different areas and all areas are important.

Each child needs some friends that he does not always have to share with his brothers and sisters. If he constantly has to play with his sister when his best friend is over he will learn to resent and think of ways to get even with her. When one of your children has a friend over, let another one have his friend with him. You will find less quarreling as they each involve themselves with their friends.

It is wise to keep in mind that in play groups, even-numbered groups do better than odd-numbered groups. When three children are playing, inevitably, two will gang up against the other. It may not always be possible to set up even-numbered groups, so activities will need to be planned and changed according to the age of the children.

A child needs time alone with each of his parents. This will take some planning, but it is so important to help children feel good about each other. Shared activities are necessary for the mental well-being of the family, but each child needs mom and dad alone, even if for only one hour a week. I know one father whose job necessitates traveling. Time at home is very limited for him, but once a week he takes one child out to lunch or dinner alone. There are four children and each gets one turn a month. Oh, how they look forward to that turn! That is their special time with dad.

What can we do when quarrels are in full swing? Must we always end up screaming, and hitting in our roles as referees? Try not to interfere in your children's quarrels. Teach your children to solve their own problems; "I'm sorry you are so upset with your brother. I'm sure the two of you can work things out to settle the problem." Interfere only if you see danger. Then, separate the children until feelings calm down. Time-out is good for this. This strategy takes lots of will power but it does work if you use it consistently. At family planning meetings you might discuss alternative ways to settle disagreements so your children can learn how to handle their feelings. They need to learn how to channel their feelings, talk problems out, and how to compromise. This takes a childhood to learn.

Try to step in before the children begin quarreling. They may be bored or tired. A different activity, a story or a favorite tv program may do the trick. Having an older child do a favor for you might be just what is needed; "I need your help with this drawer. It's stuck. You do such a fine job helping me. Would you help me now?"

Have your children perform their activities at different times. This will necessitate creativity on your part, but it is well worth the effort. Have one child build his block structure when the younger one is taking her nap. This will avoid the block structure being knocked down by the younger child. Be sure, if little children are around, projects are built on tables or put on high shelves.

Guide your child into developing interests of his own. Each boy in your family may not want to be a boy scout. Each child needs to feel he can develop his own interests without feeling inferior to another brother or sister. Observe your child. Talk about what interests him. His teacher may give you some ideas. Then help him explore his interest.

Do not make your love conditional. Love each of your children for who they are. You may not like what they have done, but they need to know that no matter how they have failed they have your love.

Getting together often in family planning meetings and discussing feelings of family members will help to bring emotions out into the open. Be sure each member has a chance to talk without interruption. Smoldering feelings tend to lead to problems. Talk about privileges and family responsibilities. This will help them feel more a part of the family. Try to be as fair as possible, but remember we are human and nothing in life is exact. Just try to do your best.

Fairness is a topic of great concern to children. Children can learn to move from selfishness to selflessness, but it is a slow process that even some adults never achieve. Teach your children that you cannot always be exactly fair, but that you are trying to the best of your ability.

Next time your children begin arguing over who has more breakfast cereal, have them count out the cereal piece by piece. They will soon tire of this and exclaim, "What's the difference?"

When upset and trying to win you on their side, they come running to you, have them sit down and draw a picture, or write about what happened, so you will better understand. These methods will help children handle their feelings and begin to solve their problems, rather than come to you. When you hear quarreling and do not know what has happened, be sure you do not take sides. Separate the children or redirect the activity; "I did not see what happened, so you both will have to clean up the mess." By asking "Who did this?" you may never find out, for each will blame the other. Remember, children up to four years apart in age, are fairly matched. The four year-old provokes his eight year-old sister while she watches tv until she finally hits him. Then, he screams and you enter the picture. By loving him and scolding his older sister, he gets exactly what he wants; your attention, and a scolding for his sister. Redirect their activity without taking sides.

Proper sex education from birth will help boys live with girls and girls live with boys, and help your child feel good about his body and his sexuality. This will create better understanding in your child's future relationships with the opposite sex.

Be sure you are setting a good example for your children in the way you handle disagreements with other family members. Do you have acceptable channels for your feelings? Do you talk problems out? Do you compromise when no solution is evident? Let the child know that you have disagreements and angry feelings with other family members, but that you're also working to resolve them. This does not mean that you do not love the other members in your family. Rather, it is because you do love each other that you are working to try and solve the disagreement.

With effort on your part, your children can learn how to handle disagreements in a socially acceptable way. Instead of simply running to you, perhaps you will hear them express with concern, "It won't do any good to run to mother. She'll only tell us to solve it ourselves." As they begin to solve their problems, you, as a parent, will experience joy as you reap the harvest of the seeds you have planted.

SIBLING RIVALRY

Buzz Questions

1. Why do children quarrel? List reasons or situations that cause children to quarrel.

2. How does the position of the child in the family—oldest, middle or youngest relate to sibling rivalty?

3. What emotions do children experience when they are involved in sibling rivalry?

4. How do we as parents react to our children's quarrels? What feelings do we experience?

5. What role does jealousy play in sibling rivalry? How can we prevent it?

JEALOUSY

Jealousy is a feeling that makes us want to protect what we have. This feeling differs from envy, wanting something someone else has. Jealousy is both natural and learned. The feeling is natural, neither negative or positive. How it is handled is learned.

Love is a difficult concept to understand and to teach. Children look at love as a piece of pie. When pieces are cut and given out, soon there is no more pie. We need to help children understand that love has no limits. It is endless with infinite varieties. "I love you more than any other Susie in the world, just as I love Daddy as no other man in the world."

Because this concept is so difficult to understand:

- Jealousy is a strong feeling for many children. It won't go away and needs to be brought out into the open and managed with frankness and honesty.

- Be aware of incidents that can cause jealousy to flare up. A new baby in the family, a visiting relative, birthdays and holidays with gift-giving, or a returning parent who has been away for awhile. A little extra attention to the child at this time will reap benefits.

- Be careful not to praise a child excessively in front of his brothers and sisters. Labeling a child "good" frequently can cause jealous feelings to flare up among siblings.

- Remember, your child is an individual. Try not to compare him favorably or unfavorably with a brother or sister.

- The way our genes are put together determines our capacity for feelings. Some children are bothered more than others by jealous feelings. Recognize this and help the child to find more satisfaction than others in life, such as a friend of his own or recreation he can enjoy.

- Teach your child that there are disappointments in life. He will have to wait until his birthday, not his sister's to receive a gift.

- Try not to favor a child because he is easier for you to get along with. Work harder to be as fair as possible.

- Let your child help you with a younger sibling. Give him responsibilities so he can feel important. He can hold the baby's bottle, bring you supplies or read a story to his younger brother or sister.

- Let your child know you understand how he feels, that everyone feels jealous from time to time and you will help him with his feelings of jealousy. "I understand that you don't want Susie to live with us. You even dislike her at times, but Susie needs to be here. She is part of our family. Let's talk about what we can do to feel better about Susie."

Remember, jealousy protects boundaries. You need to teach your child how to handle his feelings about his boundaries in an acceptable way.

THE FAMILY CONSTELLATION

Every child has a position in the family; oldest, middle, youngest, or only child. This position can determine how a child will develop. Positions can change; a new baby, a foster child, a new marriage, a death or a divorce can cause the family constellation to change. We may not have control over the change, but as parents we need to know the characteristics of the various positions so we can help our children develop to their fullest potential.

Many factors determine the differences between siblings:

- Each of your children has been born into a different family. Your first child was born into a family of a mother and father. Your second child was born into a family of a mother, a father and a child, etc.

- We tend to identify with the child who is in the position we were in. You might identify one of your children with your own brother or sister whom you either liked or disliked.

- The age span of children also determines the differences between siblings. Usually, with more than four years difference, children tend to go their own way. With children closer in age there is more quarreling, but also greater attachment later in life.

- The sex of the child will change characteristics of position in the family. A girl being the oldest in a family will develop characteristics that may differ from the oldest child in the family being a boy.

The Oldest Child

The oldest child tends to be given the most responsibility—many times more than he can handle.

More is expected of him in behavior situations. "You should know better because you are older." is commonly heard in families.

He has a strong desire to be first, to be a leader. Statistics indicate successful executives who were first born exhibit this trait.

The oldest child tends to be overly sensitive and, because of the second child, may feel unloved and neglected.

He tries to regain his status by positive deeds and by following rules. If this fails he may become a problem child.

The oldest child has adults to imitate and tends to be more mature, responsible and successful in school than later children.

The Middle Child

The middle child has never had his parents alone.

He may feel pressure from always having a child "model" ahead of him.

He tries to get attention in many ways, such as teasing other siblings or breaking rules.

The middle child may have feelings of being unloved, or treated unfairly, and needs lots of self-esteem building.

He needs help in developing interests and friends of his own.

When a third child comes along he loses the baby role and may be neglected, which adds to his feelings of frustration and discouragement.

The middle child tends to be more adventurous and likes excitement more than his older brother or sister.

He will act spontaneously and not take life as seriously as an older sibling.

The Youngest Child

The youngest child is often pampered and over-protected by parents and siblings.

He learns how to manipulate, playing one member of the family off against the other.

He has decisions made for him and is given little responsibility.

He feels frustrated as he usually is not taken seriously.

The youngest child tends to be bossy and whiny in his manipulations, and attempts to runs the family.

The boy who has older sisters will have an easier time relating to girls later on in life.

The girl who has older brothers will feel secure from being well-protected and always having somebody there to help her.

The Only Child

The only child feels he is one of a kind.

Peer relationships are difficult for him. Parents need to provide ample opportunity for peer exposure.

He spends his childhood among adults and imitates their ways early in life. This can be difficult for him to cope with.

He usually enjoys his position as the center of attraction and tends to be self-interested.

Over-protection by his parents instills a feeling of insecurity in the child.

The only child learns that oftentimes he does not have to gain possessions by his own efforts, and so tends to sit back and have them given to him.

Twins

Fraternal twins will involve in sibling rivalry much the same as two siblings close together in age.

Twins will usually work out a satisfactory relationship. The passive twin will often, in his own way, get what he wants.

It is best to treat twins as individuals with interests of their own.

When rivalry develops it is best to separate twins.

With fraternal twins it may be wise to separate them early in school, although this may not be so with identical twins as they may need each other for security. It is best to observe these situations closely.

Remember, each position in the family constellation has advantages and disadvantages. Being aware of them will help you to reduce the disadvantages a child has in his role as oldest, middle, youngest, only or twin child.

BROTHER-SISTER RELATIONSHIPS

Sibling rivalry includes brothers and sisters and all the feelings involved. Disagreement among siblings is normal if all children in the family are raised as individuals. Children need to learn to settle their own disagreements within the guideline of not hurting themselves or others. Developing self-esteem in your children will help them in their interactions with their brothers and sisters.

WHAT PARENTS CAN DO TO HELP PREVENT QUARRELS:

1. Possessions are necessary to develop values in life. Every child needs a few things he does not have to share.

2. Children need space for themselves. Even a drawer of their own will do.

3. Every child needs privacy—time to be alone with himself.

4. Each child needs to feel he is good at doing something.

5. Children need friends of their own that they do not have to share.

6. In play, even-numbered groups do better than odd-numbered groups.

7. Each child needs time *alone* with his parents.

8. Personalities differ. This may cause friction.

9. Try not to interfere in quarrels unless there is immediate danger. Teach your child to solve his own disagreements.

10. Suggest a change of activity if irritability mounts up.

11. Have siblings do things at different times.

12. Help your children build up interests of their own.

13. Do not threaten your children by making your love conditional.

14. Avoid making comparisons of one child to another.

15. Try hard not to give an "easier" child more privileges.

Shared family planning and the giving of privileges as children show responsibility will lessen sibling rivalry. Teaching sexuality will help boys and girls live together now, and aid in their future interactions with other men and women.

STEPS TO HELP YOUR CHILDREN SOLVE THEIR QUARRELS

1. Establish ground rules. No one is to intentionally hurt themselves or others, physically or emotionally.

2. Provide ways for your child to channel his anger appropriately for his age: a box of newspapers to tear, wood to cut, a pillow to punch, hammer and nails to pound, play dough to mold, paper and pencil to describe or draw the incident, are a few suggestions.

3. When your children come running to you to solve their problem, stay our of it as much as possible. For example "I'm sure you can solve your own problem." They will soon learn it is no use to go running to Dad or Mom.

4. Do not always take sides with the crying child, or the youngest. Children are usually well-matched within a four year age span, and sex matters little.

5. Separate the children without taking sides and put them in time-out if they are hurting each other, or the danger of such is evident.

6. Do not reinforce name-calling by bringing attention to it. Congratulate the children each time they settle their quarrels without name-calling.

7. Discipline your feelings about the situation. Get involved with an activity while the children are quarreling so you will not interfere. Let the children know how you are feeling if the quarrel is not being resolved in an acceptable manner; "I'm really upset at the way you are handling this. You know the ground rules. You'll have to go in time-out."

8. Changing to, or suggesting, a new activity can prevent feelings from mounting further if you know the problem cannot be resolved at the time.

9. Talk about settling quarrels at family planning sessions. Give children suggestions of how to "talk out" problems together. Give them a chance to express their feelings verbally without interference or being judged.

10. Help children to understand that disagreements are normal when people live in close contact with each other, and are individuals with distinct personalities.

11. Together, plan ways that privacy and ownership of possessions can be respected. A closed door means you knock. Private possessions are off-limits unless permission is given.

12. Help your children to feel good about themselves (see Self-Esteem Unit). By feeling worthwhile and lovable, with interests of their own, they will be less likely to "pick" on each other.

13. Set a good example for your children in the way you handle disagreements with your husband or wife. Let your child know you have disagreements and angry feelings, and that you are working to resolve them. Disagreements do not mean there is no love. On the contrary, because you love each other, you will work harder to solve problems.

AGES AND CHANGES

Sibling-Peer Relationships

Infancy to 2½ years—

The family needs to adapt to the child.

At this age the child is at the solitary play level. He plays alone.

The child will treat other children as play objects.

He cannot share or wait his turn.

He is demanding if he cannot get his way; he will act out with temper tantrums.

2½ years to 6 years—

Relations will begin to improve.

The child will be progressing from the parallel-play stage, where he will play alongside other children, to the group-play stage where he will interact with siblings and peers.

The 3 year-old will interfere with an older sibling's belongings.

The 4 year-old, with his "out of bounds" behavior, tends to be rough and impatient. He resorts to lots of quarreling and physical fighting.

5 is a gentler age. He will accept any role in group play and wants to please. He enjoys younger siblings and is very empathetic toward brother and sister problems.

AGES AND CHANGES

Sibling-Peer Relationships

6 years to 10 years—

In play groups the 6 year-old tends to be bossy. He is involved in physical fighting and often teases other children. He feels he is grown up enough not to be cared for by older siblings and resents their authority.

At 7, the child enjoys playing the older sibling role. He tends to be more emphathetic to younger brothers and sisters than older ones. He is keenly aware of privileges given older siblings and this arouses jealous feelings.

At 8, the child experiences regressive behavior. There is lots of teasing and quarreling about possessions and privileges.

The 9 year-old resents being bossed, but is improving his relationships with other children. He is involved with groups and organized games and can follow rules if they are clearly stated. He is thoughtful and protective of younger siblings, and of his family in general.

10 years and older—

Physical fighting gives way to name-calling.

The older child does better with younger siblings, under 5, and those several years older than he is.

He will provoke younger siblings by teasing.

As the older child gets more involved with peer-group relationships, he will get along better with siblings.

Remember, the closer in age children are, the more quarreling is likely to take place; but the relationship will be closer in adulthood. Children more than 4 years apart tend to each go their own way.

OBSERVATIONS ON SIBLING RIVALRY

Observe your children the next time they quarrel. Try to avoid interfering in the quarrel.

1. Describe what is happening.

2. Do you know what caused the quarrel? (Up too late the night before, a sharing problem, lack of attention, etc.)

3. What feelings do you see the children expressing?

4. How do you feel as you observe the quarreling?

5. Was the quarrel resolved? In whose favor?

NOTES

*It takes both rain and sunshine
to make a rainbow*

FEELINGS &
EMOTIONS,
BUILDING POSITIVE
MENTAL HEALTH

FEELINGS AND EMOTIONS

"Feelings always affect your body and your body always affects your feelings. They are all one. Feelings influence just about everything we do. They affect the way we think about ourselves and about other people. They affect the way we behave."
Eda Le Shan, **What Makes Me Feel This Way?**

Along with physical health, we need mental well-being. Positive mental health means being able to handle our feelings and emotions in ways that do not interfere with friendships, work, or our ability to do what we are capable of doing. Feelings and emotions play an important part of our mental well-being. They constitute the overall quality of our awareness. Our bodies are made up of many feelings and emotions. All of them are important to make up the total us. Sometimes feelings are very difficult to distinguish. Can you remember feeling angry about something and yet realizing that anger was really covering up another feeling? Perhaps you were disappointed over something one of your children did and you began to lash out at them in anger.

You are made up of many feelings. Take a piece of paper and list as many feelings as possible that you have experienced. Did you find that you were listing things such as anger, fear, depression, revenge, and resentment on one side of the paper, and feelings such as joy, happiness, sympathy, love on another side of the paper? Feelings are not negative or positive in themselves. All feelings are in us for a reason. They make up the total us. What we are held accountable for are the reactions to those feelings. Those become either positive or negative.

Tension and anxiety are feelings that are difficult to separate. Tension is the disturbed and upset feeling you get when your body mobilizes to deal with a real threat. Anxiety is the uneasy feeling you get in anticipation or expectation of a threat. For example, when your child is not on the school bus at 4:00 P.M., you begin to feel anxious. All kinds of questions pop into your mind and you begin to expect the worse. The phone rings and your friend tells you that your child is over at her house. He has missed the bus and you need to pick him up. You feel relieved. Then you begin to feel tension, because now you must solve the problem of how to pick him up as you remember that you don't have the car today. You need to determine what you will do to remedy this situation.

Today's society often triggers the feeling of anxiety. On a piece of paper list all the things that happen to you in your day that make you feel anxious. Did you list such things as money, job or work, sex, appearance, safety and health? Now, make another list. List the happenings that occur in the day that cause you to be anxious because you are a parent. Did you list such things as education, your child's peer group, money, safety, health and nutrition? Now, pretend you are a child. Think about the pressures that happen to a child during the day that cause him to be anxious. How about parents, school, and friends? If your child is a teenager, how about sex, drugs and appearance?

Even if we have all of these pressures daily, something can be done to help us channel our feelings as we go through the day. One way we can channel feelings is to exercise. Whether it's playing tennis or going for a walk, exercise is very important in helping to release the built-up energy feelings create.

Sleeping and eating habits play a role in channeling feelings. People require different amounts of sleep. Some can get by on as little as four hours of sleep a night and some require eight or more. Your child will set his own pattern if you guide him and provide the proper environment.

Eating habits are important, also. We need balanced diets to stay healthy. Successful research is being done that connects diet with behavior problems. A high sugar content releases energy quickly instead of keeping the energy level high, as protein does, for longer periods of time. Tiredness takes over in a relatively short period of time, not enabling a child to handle his feelings effectively. If our bodies are healthy, we are better able to handle our feelings.

The least amount of pills or medication will help us keep our bodies functioning properly. Medications can cause allergies or addiction or can be very dangerous, especially when driving. Follow your doctor's prescriptions, but, try not to rely on medication for your well-being.

We all need time by ourselves. Children need time alone, also. It's important that we get to know ourselves. We need time away from people and problems around us. We need to be doing something we like to do by ourselves.

Recognizing physical symptoms, such as headaches, stomach cramps and heart palpitations that are caused by not releasing our feelings, is important, and many times overlooked. Our body is trying to tell us that something is wrong. Children have warnings also, but may not be aware of what they mean. Watch for signs such as nervous movements of the shoulders, eyes or head, nail-biting or nightmares at night. These signs tell us that we need to help our children slow down.

Avoiding boredom, and developing hobbies and interests, helps channel our feelings into acceptable outlets. We need to have hobbies and interests, and we need to help our children develop their own interests. These interests will help make the daily routine of life bearable and joyful.

Another way to release feelings and emotions is to talk about them. It is important that we have someone to talk to about how we are feeling. Your child needs to talk to you. Listen to him without being judgmental; "What do you mean you hate school? You're going anyway." A nonjudgmental statement will help your child handle his feelings and not shut off communication; "Sounds as if you're unhappy about school. Let's talk about it."

Lastly, we can organize time. By having our time organized, not necessarily minute by minute, we will find that we have more time for ourselves and more time to do some of the things that we want to do without feeling so pressured.

There are some important facts that we need to keep in mind about feelings and emotions. Remember that feelings are neither positive or negative. It is the reaction to feelings that we label positive or negative and that we are held responsible for.

Emotions are related to our temperament. The capacities of feelings differ in each individual. You and I are both bothered by the feeling of jealousy and yet because of the way our genes are put together, I may have a more difficult time coping with my feeling of jealousy. It may "flare" up inside me at the slightest incident but only "glow" inside you. This is why one child in your family might have so much trouble with the feeling of jealousy and another child is hardly bothered at all by this feeling. Of course, environmental factors will enter in, such as the position in the family, a crisis or self-image.

We know that emotions and feelings are linked through our nervous system to the entire biological system. The two cannot really be separated, so when our feelings are kept inside, they are bound to erupt somewhere in our body, as a headache or a nervous twitch or an ulcer. You need to be familiar with your individual emotional strengths and weaknesses. Know where your "breaking point" is.

Keep in mind that feelings and emotions are often mixed together and can be very confusing, hard to get in touch with, and difficult to separate. This is important to remember when we are trying to help our children get in touch with their feelings.

There are unhealthy attitudes about feelings that we all have heard. For example, a common belief is that the expression of feelings should be hidden or denied, especially in men. It is not very masculine for a man to cry, but we know that men have feelings as well as women. We encourage this attitude many times as parents by saying such things as, "Little boys don't cry" or "Big boys aren't afraid of anything. Do you want to grow up to be a sissy?" We need to be careful in mentioning such statements to our children because these statements will orientate them toward a negative way of handling their feelings and emotions.

Another unhealthy attitude that has been around for awhile is that repression of feelings is a sign of humility. To be humble is to acknowledge feelings as part of our being and to admit to all our feelings, realizing they all are an enrichment to life, not to ignore and repress them as something evil.

Be prepared for the consequences of your emotions and teach your child to accept the responsibility for his feelings. If emotions and feelings are not released in ways that are socially acceptable, then we must be prepared to accept and handle the consequences.

Guilt should not be a result of a feeling we are experiencing. Morally we are held accountable for the action we channel our feelings into. It is not wrong to feel angry, but it is wrong to channel that anger into hurting yourself or another person. This is difficult for children to understand until they are able to develop morality and form values—until that time, they will learn this concept by imitating you.

When a situation occurs there is not an immediate reaction on our part to that situation. We are in charge of our feelings, and we need to be in touch with them and then respond to them. In between situation A and the reaction C, we experience a feeling and do what we call "self-talk." All of us will talk to ourselves before we react. How we talk to ourselves will determine how we will react. For example, you are having a party. You have been planning this for a long time and you are hoping everyone will have a good time. Your four year-old comes into the room and yells, "I hate all these people and I want them to go home!" How are you feeling? Before you act you will be doing some "self talk." You could feel rejection. "He doesn't love me. How could he do this to me?" Or you could feel revenge, "I'll show him. How dare he hurt me like this!" Or you might feel compassion and say to yourself, "Poor fellow, he's really being ignored. I'll have to explain to him I don't like what he is doing and show him how he can get my attention in an acceptable way." Your self-talk will determine how you will react in the above situation. You are in charge of your feelings and self-talk. It is important for us to learn skills to have our self-talk be as logical as possible.

Children's anxious feelings usually show up as fears. The feeling of fear tends to be at a height between the ages of two and six. This is during the "imaginary" stage we talked about in Growth and Development. Nighttime seems to be worse because darkness is an unknown, and we tend to be fearful of the unknown. Be careful never to force a child to face a fear. He needs to do this gradually. We want our children to be cautious in life, recognizing dangers, but being able to live with them, rather than fearful, which can result in a paralyzing withdrawal from life. A child who has a satisfactory relationship with both parents has the best chance to deal with his fears.

Fears may differ with the ages of children. Preschoolers may be afraid of an injury to their body or think they may flush down the toilet or go down the bathtub drain with the bath water. Separation from parents is one of the greatest fears of preschoolers. This is why a preschooler is always asking, "Do you love me?" He needs constant reassurance that you do.

An elementary school aged child may be fearful of school situations, perhaps afraid of failing. He may be afraid that he won't be accepted by his peer group. The teenager again will have fears. School, peers, parents and society can all cause anxieties in teenagers that lead to fears. Emancipation probably is the greatest fear the teenager may experience.

Children tend to handle fears in their own way. Play is one way that they handle fears. When you watch children at play, they are acting out the feelings they have. Have you ever seen children acting out a burial? Perhaps a pet of theirs has died, and they are very fearful. Not only do they miss their pet, but they wonder if "dying" will happen to them. They are trying to handle death in their play.

Older children, through their team games and vigorous exercise, will be handling feelings such as fear, trying to channel this feeling into an acceptable outlet. We need to remember that all of us have fears of one sort or another. We may not completely eradicate that fear, but we need to learn to live with that fear so that it will not interfere with our daily living.

Close contact with you is important to help children feel secure and help them to handle their feelings. They need to talk them out. By talking out their fears, they will begin to learn to live with them. Listen to your child. He is telling you so much. Watch for clues to help you understand what his fears are.

Prepare your child for something that might be frightening. Visit the dentist *before* he needs dental work. How do you handle your fears? If you run under the bed when a thunderstorm hits, he will also tend to do the same. How are you preparing your child to handle his fears?

If your child is afraid of something, try to talk about it. Study it. If you have a fear of the same thing, have someone close to you help you both. For example, if he has a fear of spiders, you might want to get a book from the library on spiders to learn more about them. Collect a few spiders. Watch one spin a web. Your child will become fascinated by this and while learning he will be conquering his fear, at least well enough to be able to live side by side with spiders in this world.

Never use fear as discipline. "If you don't behave in this store, I'm calling that policeman over there and he'll put you in jail." Your child may stop his behavior, but he is building up fears that may take a lifetime to eradicate. Give him a correct reason why he needs to behave in a certain way.

Be careful not to expect too much from your child whether at home or at school. Pressure put on him to overachieve causes anxieties which can be expressed as fears. Let him achieve at his own rate of growth and development.

There are other ways you can help your child with his fears. Be careful of his entertainment. Television and ghost stories can frighten children. Act as a "level" for your child. Talk about what he is seeing and hearing. "Lassie" may be a fine show for eleven and twelve year-olds, but much too emotional for a five or six year-old.

Be sure your child can trust you. Call when you are late coming home. Be sure you try to come home when you say you will. This will also help to teach your child to do the same when he is out.

Do not keep your child dependent on you. He can't learn to do for himself and he'll be fearful of new experiences. Remember you are raising your child to leave you. The more he can do for himself, the more capable he will feel and, as a result, he'll have less anxieties and fears.

There are times when children will try to manipulate you. They will use their feelings, such as fear or anger or love, to make you do what they want you to do. A child who shows fear when you arrive later than you anticipated can scream and carry on in such a manner that you wouldn't dare be late one minute. By accommodating your child in this manner, he is manipulating you to be home when he says so. If he is fearful and you know you may be late, call to reassure him. Have a neighbor check on him. If the child is old enough give him a key, or tell him where a key will be hidden so he can get into the house. Make preparations ahead of time.

Anger can be used to manipulate parents. Most parents will do anything the child wants when out in public. A child, kicking and screaming in a library because he wants a certain book, may put the parent in an embarrassing situation. Everyone is looking. It is so much easier to give him the book to quiet him down rather than to remove him from the library until he quiets down. Giving in to the child only reinforces this behavior to happen again.

Children will threaten to withhold love from their parents to get what they want. Here again, no parent wants to be told he isn't loved by his child. It hurts, yet to give in shows the child what a powerful weapon he has. Try to recognize the situation for what it is. Be sure what you are asking is reasonable, then discipline the child positively. He needs to learn that feelings should not be used to manipulate people if he is to establish positive relationships with them.

Children are often frightened by the way they feel. Sometimes their feelings are all mixed up. How can I love one minute and hate the next? What is wrong with me? Why do I sometimes hate and love at the same time? You need to talk to your child about feelings and emotions and let him know we all feel this way at one time or another. Help him learn the ground rule that it is all right to feel anger or any other feeling, and that he needs to express this feeling, but he cannot express his feelings in a way that would hurt himself, others, or destroy property. It is all right for him to punch a pillow, but not to hit you. Making playdough, baking, chopping wood, tearing newspaper in a box might all be ways your child can handle his angry feelings that will be acceptable.

We know that children whose basic needs are satisfied are better able to be in touch with their feelings and not let them interfere in their daily living. Children need to feel that they are loved—that people close to them want them, care for them, love them very much. They need to feel worthwhile and accepted. They need to have a positive self-image. If they feel that they are accepted just the way they are, they will better be able to handle their feelings. All children need to feel secure. They need to know that they have a place, a home, that is secure and safe and that their parents will always be around to help them. They need to feel protected, that someone will help them and keep them safe from harm, that when they have to face an unknown situation, someone will be there to help them.

Children need to develop independence. They need to know that their parents want them to grow and mature and to eventually emancipate themselves. They need to feel that their parents will teach them responsibility. They will soon learn that privileges come with responsibilities, and with privileges and responsibilities, independence is evident.

Children also need to develop a set of moral standards to live by. They need a belief in human values, such as kindness, courage, generosity and honesty. They also need a belief in spiritual values, to know that there is a divine power and to develop a faith in that power. Children need guidance to learn how to behave towards persons and things, to know there are limits to what they are permitted to do and that their parents will hold them to those limits. Even though it is all right to feel jealous or angry, they will not be allowed to hurt themselves or others or destroy property when they have those feelings.

Your four year-old child is afraid of the dark. Every night he cries and cries and cannot fall asleep. What are some of the things you might do to help him? You might want to play some games in the dark, not at the time he is going to bed, but at another time. You can sit with him a little while before bedtime and read him a pleasant story—not something that would be frightening. Leave a night light on in his room or a light in the bathroom close by, so he can see it. Not only will it help him with his fear, but it is also a safety precaution. Let him spend a night outdoors with you, sleeping in a tent in your backyard. Look at the stars together and listen to the quietness of the evening. This will help him to have a warm feeling about darkness and night. Give him a flashlight of his own that he can keep under his pillow. He might be using it the first time a little too much, but after a while, the novelty will wear off, and he'll feel confident that if a shadow flashes across the wall and he thinks it's a monster, he can turn his flashlight on and feel secure.

Your seven year-old is frightened of failing in school. You notice that he is having nightmares at night. What can you do as a parent to help him? Give him a little extra help with his homework. Provide a quiet study time for him with few distractions. If he asks a question, be there to answer it. Ask the teacher what you can do to help. Teachers are usually willing to help and can give you advice on how to help at home. Try to build your child's confidence. Praise him when he accomplishes a task that he can do with ease. Let him know you are there to help. Games will help in some subjects, such as math or reading. Playing cards is an excellent way to help a child learn numbers and they love to play cards.

Your teenager is having difficulty making friends. What can you do to help him? Try to build his confidence. Let him know he is important in your eyes. Praise him for things he does around home and praise him for his appearance. Invite other teenagers over. Be sure he knows he can have someone sleep over or give a party occasionally. You might ask friends over who have teenagers his age. By just putting teenagers in close proximity, communication begins. Plan an outing where he will be around teenage children. Perhaps a new outfit that you both can save together for will give him that confidence he needs. Appearance is important to feeling good.

Our support as parents can do much to help our children handle their feelings and emotions and to make them feel good about themselves. When they feel good about themselves, we will experience joy as we see them develop into mature adults, capable of handling their feelings and emotions in a way that does not interfere with their daily living.

Help each family member get in touch with his feelings and enjoy doing it. Give each one a piece of paper and some crayons. Have them sit on the floor with plenty of room around them to work. Have each one think back to the last time he was angry. Where did it happen, who was around? Can you remember the people involved? What incident just occurred to make you feel angry? Where do you feel the anger? Is it in your stomach? Do you feel it in your head? Or the back of your neck? Do your hands feel tense? Now, take that feeling and put it on paper. You may use colors, lines, and circles to express your feeling instead of figures. Try to put down on paper just how you are feeling.

Choose another feeling, such as love. When was the last time that you felt really loving. Who were the people involved? What just happened? Where do you feel that feeling of love? Is it in your stomach? Do you feel it in your head or do you feel it throughout your body? Now, take a piece of paper and try to draw that feeling. When you are finished, have each member in your family talk about those feelings and let them tell how they described it on paper. This exercise can be done with any feeling that we experience. Sometimes their feelings may be difficult to separate and they will express two or three feelings in their drawing. These exercises will help each of the members of your family to get in touch with their feelings, to be aware of them and to realize that the physical is so closely connected with the emotional.

Remember that feelings are part of us. What we do with our feelings for our mental well-being is learned. Our children need to learn how to handle their feelings. If they can handle their feelings in a way that is acceptable to them and to others, they will feel good about themselves and others, and they will experience joy as they interact with life.

FEELINGS AND EMOTIONS

1. Feelings and emotions are neither positive or negative. They make up the total us. Only consequences of our feelings and emotions can be judged positively or negatively.

2. Feelings and emotions are related to temperament. Capacities differ according to the way our genes are put together. Expression of our feelings is learned. There should be no guilt connected with feelings, only with actions as a result of emotions.

3. Feelings and emotions are linked to the biological system. This is why physical ailments such as headaches, stomach pains, high blood pressure and heart problems can be attributed to improper expression of emotions. Every time you or your child are angry or frightened:

   - Your heart beats faster.
   - Digestion slows down.
   - Blood rushes to outer limbs.
   - There is a stimulation of the liver and sweat glands.
   - Pupils of the eyes dilate to let in more vision.
   - Coagulation of the blood is increased.

4. Feelings and emotions need to be expressed by both men and women.

5. We need to admit to all feelings and emotions.

6. Watch for signs of your emotional weaknesses. Help your child recognize his symptoms; nailbiting, irritability, stomachaches and bedwetting can be signs of emotional disturbance.

7. Help your child learn how to handle his feelings.

   - Exercise
   - Good sleeping and eating habits
   - Minimal medication as possible
   - Time alone
   - Developing a hobby or interest
   - Organize time better
   - Talk about feelings
   - Help your child to get in touch with and handle his feelings and emotions by letting him know it is all right to have the feeling and giving him alternatives to express that feeling. "I know you are angry with me. You can't hit me, but you can punch this pillow."

8. Crisis such as divorce, death, moving, a new baby, and non-acceptance from peers will trigger emotions. Be sure to provide outlets for your child or these suppressed feelings will cause problems.

SOME FEELINGS AND EMOTIONS WE ALL EXPERIENCE

Love
Jealousy
Joy
Hate
Revenge
Sympathy
Empathy
Depression
Guilt
Envy
Disgust
Happiness
Fear
Satisfaction
Sexuality
Frustration
Failure
Success
Pity
Wonder
Resentment
Inferiority
Superiority
Grief
Surprise
Yearning
Awe

Rage
Anxiety
Tension
Hurt
Disappointment
Encouragement
Challenge
Courage
Kindness
Helpfulness
Honesty
Hunger
Sleepiness
Uncomfortableness
Laziness
Sloppiness
Neatness
Warmth
Curiosity
Pain
Loneliness
Despair
Hope
Romance
Desperation
Security
Comfort

YOUR CHILD'S FEARS

Children have anxious feelings. These usually are expressed as fears. Fear is a paralyzing withdrawal. Caution is recognition of dangers and handling them in such a way so as not to interfere with daily living.

Fear is at its height between two and six years of age. Nighttime is worst. A child with satisfactory relationships to both parents has the best chance to deal with his fears and overcome them.

As a parent you can help your child with his fears:

1. Prepare your child for something that might be frightening, such as a visit to the dentist prior to the actual dental work.

2. Your example in dealing with fears will teach him how to handle his.

3. Never use fear as discipline, "If you don't sit down in this car, I'll call that policeman over."

4. Do not expect too much of your child in school.

5. Avoid humiliation, "Big boys aren't afraid of the dark."

6. Don't be indifferent to fears. They are real and need to be handled.

7. Be careful of movies, television, ghost stories and teasing.

8. Help him distinguish between what is real and what is imaginary.

9. Be sure your child can trust you. Come home when you say you will, or call if that is impossible.

10. Do not keep a child dependent on you. He can't learn to do for himself and will be fearful of new experiences.

11. Know when your child is using his fear to manipulate you, for example, not wanting to go to bed at night after all necessities are taken care of.

12. Listen to your child. Observe him for clues to his fears. Once you know them, you'll be able to help him with them.

FEELINGS AND EMOTIONS

Buzz Questions

1. List fears that children have.

       Two—six year-olds—

       Seven—twelve year-olds—

       Thirteen—eighteen year-olds—

2. How do children show their fears?

3. List ways children handle their fears.

4. Children need to be taught that feelings and emotions need to be expressed and channeled into acceptable outlets. What would be acceptable to you for the following feelings?

anger   sadness
love   excitement
jealousy   fear
happiness   sympathy

MANIPULATION

Feelings and emotions can be manipulative. Adults, as well as children try to get their way by using feelings. Such tactics as withholding love or sex, crying, and temper tantrums are common. When given in to, these actions are reinforced and so continue. They need to be ignored.

Fear— Your child is afraid of the dark. This is a real fear, a fear of the unknown. Be supportive of your child. Keep a night light on, read to him before bedtime, let him know you will be close by. Then leave his room. If he tries to leave, put him back. He may be crying and this may go on for several hours. Be firm, but supportive. Soon he will realize that he will have to live with his fear and try to work it out for himself.

Anger—Anger is a secondary feeling. Usually it covers up another feeling. Children express anger in many ways just as adults do. They may be frightened by not understanding why they feel angry. Reassure them that it is all right to feel angry but they cannot hurt themselves or others. Your child is having a temper tantrum. He is kicking and screaming. The more you plead with him, the more attention you are giving him. Temper tantrums are for audiences. Once you make sure he cannot hurt himself or someone else, walk away. He will soon stop. Then give him something else to do to show what is permissible and praise him if he responds.

Love—Children can learn to manipulate parents by withholding love. Your first reaction to your child's words, "I hate you" is self-pity. A feeling of hurt goes through you. Remember, he is talking about the power you have over him. Don't take it personally. "I'm sorry you are feeling that way now. I often feel that way too. You'll feel better later." This will not allow the child to manipulate you and also lets him know that there is nothing wrong with him if he has this feeling.

Remember, children will continue to manipulate you with their feelings if their actions are reinforced. If they see manipulation among adults, they will tend to imitate it. Children need to learn to get in touch with their feelings and to be honest about them. They have to learn this from you.

WHAT CHILDREN NEED FOR POSITIVE MENTAL HEALTH

Positive mental health means being able to handle your feelings and emotions in a way that does not interfere with your daily life; work or interactions with people.

Children whose basic needs are satisfied are better able to be in touch with their feelings, not let them interfere with their daily living.

LOVE
Children need to feel they are lovable, that their parents love, want and enjoy them; that they matter very much to someone; that there are people near them who care what happens to them. Children need to feel worthwhile; that they can do something well; that they can have time for themselves and that they can have goals they can accomplish.

ACCEPTANCE
Children need to believe they are accepted; that their parents like them for themselves, just the way they are; that they like them all the time, and not only when they act according to their ideas of the way children should act; that they always accept them even though they often may not approve of the things they do, and that they will let them grow and develop in their own way as an individual.

SECURITY
Children need to feel secure that their home is a good, safe place they can feel sure about; that their parents will always be on hand, especially in time of crisis when they need them the most and that they belong to a family or group; that there is a place where they fit in.

PROTECTION

Children need to feel protected; that their parents will keep them safe from harm; that they will help them when they must face strange, unknown and frightening situations, and that they will recognize their fears and not humiliate or embarrass them.

INDEPENDENCE

Children need to develop independence. They need to know that their parents want them to grow up and that they encourage them to try new things; that they have confidence in them and in their ability to do things for themselves and by themselves; that they will give them responsibility so they can earn privileges and that they will let them make mistakes and help them learn from them.

FAITH

Children need to develop a set of moral standards to live by; a belief in the human values—kindness, courage, honesty, generosity and justice.

GUIDANCE

Children need to have friendly help in learning how to behave toward persons and things; grownups around them who show them by example how to get along with others; that there are limits to what they are permitted to do and that their parents will hold them to these limits; that though it is all right to feel jealous and angry, they will not be allowed to hurt themselves or others when they have these feelings.

WHEN TO SEEK PROFESSIONAL HELP

Professional help is available through churches, agencies, schools, medical clinics, and mental health clinics. Be sure you use these facilities if you suspect the following:

1. Unresponsiveness from your baby. His eyes do not follow movement. He does not react to loud noises. He doesn't try to imitate your facial expression such as a smile.

2. Repeated aggressive behavior. He has a pattern of hurting himself, hurting others, or destroying property.

3. A tendency to withdraw from life by shutting others out or by not meeting problems head-on.

4. He is depressed or unhappy most of the time.

5. Continuous nightmares may be a sign to seek help. A child may express anxious feelings with fears. Watch for this in his daily routine.

6. Frequent complaining of stomach aches or headaches or other physical symptoms.

7. Failure syndrome in school. Once a failure pattern is established, help is usually needed to break the cycle.

8. Bedwetting after school age. Remember, however, that there is a tendency for bedwetting to be in the family tree.

9. If your child has repeated episodes of running away, counseling will help your child and you.

10. It is fine for a child to have one or two friends or many, but if you notice difficulty in making or keeping friends as a frequent pattern, seek help.

11. Any extreme change of behavior pattern is a sign to seek outside help.

12. Be sure you are looking at these behavior patterns for intensity and frequency. One or two episodes such as bedwetting does not necessarily mean help is needed. When in doubt, ask.

Remember, positive mental health is as important as good physical health. The two are inseparable.

BRINGING UP MENTALLY
HEALTHY CHILDREN

Rate yourself from 1 (less frequently) to 5 (more frequently) on the following parent checklist.

1. Do you encourage your child by praising him for behavior that is acceptable to you?

   _____

2. Do you often laugh at his mistakes?

   _____

3. Do you compare your child with other children in the family or with his friends?

   _____

4. Do you kiss, hug and fondle him excessively?

   _____

5. Do you believe that the first consideration in the home shall always be the child's and not the parent's?

   _____

6. If your child has a terrifying experience, would you encourage him to talk about it?

_____

7. Do you give him excessive attention when he is ill?

_____

8. Do you attempt to protect your child from all situations which have a degree of danger in them?

_____

9. Have you acquired the habit of speaking to him pleasantly?

_____

10. Do you interfere when he has a quarrel with a friend?

_____

11. Do you show-off your child frequently before company?

_____

12. Does he feel free to confide in you?

_____

13. Do you assign tasks and responsibilities together as a family? (Taking care of clothes, toys, duties about home, etc.)

_____

14. Do you use fear instead of reason in disciplining? (i.e. "If you don't sit down I'll call that policeman," or "If you don't take your medicine, I'll take you to the doctor for a shot.") _____

15. Do you encourage your child to play with children of his own age? _____

16. Do you bribe your child with a present or a treat in order to make him behave? _____

17. Do you interfere when your husband (or wife) is disciplining him? _____

18. Do you explain to your child in an understanding way what you expect of him? _____

19. When your child appears happy at the idea of going somewhere without you, do you feel hurt? _____

20. Do you permit your child to make certain decisions, for example, concerning clothes and food? _____

21. Do you give in to your child when he has a temper tantrum?

_____

22. Does your child have the proper amount of rest daily to keep him from being irritable?

_____

23. At mealtime, is the food placed before him without comment?

_____

24. Is your child permitted to eat much or little without any forcing, pleading or reminding?

_____

25. Are both parents co-partners in the rearing of the child?

_____

26. Does your child have a regular routine of sleeping, eating, health habits and play?

_____

27. Are you more lenient with him when you are in a good mood?

_____

28. If your child is very much afraid of something, do you force him to meet the situation?

_____

29. Do you order your child never to fight or resist, if he is attacked by another child?

_____

30. Do you display over-anxiety concerning your child's health and take extreme precautions lest he contract illnesses?

                  _____

31. Are mother and father well-mated and does love and harmony exist between them?

                  _____

32. Do you answer simply and truthfully his questions on sex?

                  _____

33. Does your child feel that he is really wanted and that you will always love him?

                  _____

34. Does your child have a place, which he can call his own—a room or corner?

                  _____

35. Have you provided your child with materials which stimulate self-expression, i.e. clay, blocks, crayons, paints, brushes, paper, etc.?

                  _____

36. Do you label your child as "impossible," "awful," "devil," "stupid" or "good"?

                  _____

37. Is the home broken up because of divorce or separation of parents?

                  _____

38. Has the mother any wholesome interests which necessitate her getting away from the children occasionally?

_____

39. Do both mother and father show genuine interest in the various activities of the child?

_____

40. Do you put off punishing your child when he needs it and insist that your partner assume the responsibility?

_____

CHILDREN LEARN WHAT THEY LIVE

If a child lives with criticism.   He learns to condemn.

If a child lives with hostility.   He learns to fight.

If a child lives with ridicule.   He learns to be shy.

If a child lives with shame.   He learns to feel guilty.

If a child lives with tolerance.   He learns to be patient.

If a child lives with encouragement.   He learns confidence.

If a child lives with praise.   He learns to appreciate.

If a child lives with fairness.   He learns justice.

If a child lives with security.   He learns to have faith.

If a child lives with approval.   He learns to like himself.

If a child lives with acceptance and friendship.   He learns to find
love in the world.

Dorothy Law Nolte

NOTES

Parenting is like an onion,
you peel off one layer
at a time and sometimes
you weep

SEXUALITY, MORALITY & VALUES

SEXUALITY, MORALITY AND VALUES

"Parents are the sex educators of their own children, whether they do it well or badly. Silence and evasiveness are just as powerful teachers as are the facts . . ."

Sexuality is the whole self of male or femaleness. There is more to sex than just doing it. It is a part of growth and development, part of our personality, a part of living and a part of love. It constitutes identification of a male with males, female with females and includes the attraction of male and female. Positive sexuality means living comfortably with sex and feeling good about ourselves so we can feel good about others. This is the sign of a mature adult.

Why do we need to teach sexuality? We need to educate the whole child; intellectually: physically, emotionally, socially, sexually and spiritually. The child is made up of an intellect and body with emotions and feelings. He lives among people and needs to learn how to interact socially with them. To neglect one area of this development is not to develop a total human being. God created male and female, and sexually they live together as part of His plan. Spiritually, children need to recognize God as a power beyond material being.

Because of our backgrounds and upbringing, we may have "hang ups" about our ideas of sex. Can you remember some of the "locker room" talk that you honestly believed and worried about? If you masturbate, hair will grow on the palms of your hands; you are fragile during menstruation; the size of your penis determines if you will enjoy sex; you can get pregnant by kissing, etc. How relieved you felt when you found out these things were not true. So many of our feelings about sex have been carried over to adulthood. Without education, they remain and cause problems in our relationships with the opposite sex.

Today everything about sex is out in the open. Our children are faced with this from early age on. Television commercials portray the ideal woman and man. If you smell good, you'll find romance. Magazines and advertisements, from selling cars to buying groceries, portray sex.

Look through a common household magazine. Tear out every picture that denotes sexuality. This will give you an idea of what your children are looking at. Exposure to information can be positive, but it can also be negative if we feel that appearance is what makes a fulfilled person. Our self-image is lowered because we cannot fit the so called "norm" of a physically beautiful man or woman. Children need us to interpret what is the realistic norm of a fulfilled life and what is not.

We believe in long lasting marriages, but statistics prove otherwise. What is happening? Sexuality includes feelings and emotions and responsibility to our partner, along with sex. We need to help our children understand this. Sex information alone will not teach this. Values enter in.

Venereal disease is in epidemic stages throughout the United States and emotional problems of pregnant teenagers and unwed mothers soar. Is sex education necessary? One need only look at the statistics to be assured that it is.

Parents are the primary educators of children, but because many parents are not fulfilling this responsibility for one reason or another and because education at home, to be effective, must be reinforced, schools, churches and the community need to be involved. Teenagers can discuss sexuality in a peer group with a trained leader easier than with their own parents. Why not take advantage of this? Teen "rap" sessions in schools and churches can teach correct sex information and reinforce values such as truth, honesty and integrity. Get involved as a parent.

Find out what your child's school is teaching about sexuality. See what is happening in your church and community.

Children learn sexuality from the time of conception. The warmth and security of the womb reassures the new little life. After birth, mother's touch, cuddling, bathing, and gentle carresses feel pleasurable and are teaching that baby that he is a worthwhile and lovable being. Toilet training is an important stage of life that carries over into sexuality. Slow, patient, non-pressurized guidance at this time is important to help your child feel good about himself. I know of no time when you are an adult that it is important when you were "potty trained." The question has never been on a job application.

Husband and wife attitudes toward each other teach their children sexuality. The nicest thing you can do for your children is to love your partner. How you feel about yourself teaches sexuality. If you feel good about yourself, you will be able to feel good about your partner and your children.

Each member in your family needs privacy, a place and time away from everyone. Teach your child to knock on a closed door and you do the same. His private world needs to be his own.

The concept that children learn sexuality from nudity leaves much to be desired. If you feel comfortable running around the house nude, your children will accept that, but when your children reach puberty their feelings and emotions are difficult for them to cope with, so cover up. If you are more comfortable dressed, fine. On the other hand, if your children accidentally see you with no clothes on, don't fall apart. A simple, "Oops, someone forgot to knock" will not leave your child with the impression that something is drastically wrong with the human body.

You can teach sexuality to your child. Help your child become familiar with his body. Name parts of his body while bathing, but be sure to use correct names. A kindergarten teacher told me of her plight when she was teaching a new class of youngsters. One little girl kept coming up to her and telling her she had to "whisper." When no whispering came, she sent the child back to her table. Soon there was a flood on the floor. Whisper meant urinate, as this teacher soon learned. Be sure your child knows correct bathroom language before school age.

Teach your child respect for his body, not to injure it in any way so he can learn to respect others. Sex denotes responsibility. We are responsible for our sexual actions. Start early with this. Boys need to be just as responsible for their actions as girls. Usually, the burden is placed on the girl because she becomes pregnant. The boy is as responsible, and both boy and girl need to face the consequences of their act.

Help your child feel good about himself by providing an environment that will develop a positive self image. Give him responsibility and independence. Praise him for behavior you approve. Let him know he is a capable and lovable person.

Satisfy your child's curiosity. Read books to him geared to his age level. If he has no sisters, let him babysit a baby girl so he can learn that girls are "different" than boys, and that they are supposed to be different. Brothers and sisters can bath together occasionally at an early age so a little boy doesn't have to worry that he will lose his penis "like his sister did." Or a little girl does not have to worry that "she is missing something."

Be sure you give correct information. If you don't know an answer, look it up. Give simple answers and start early. If your child doesn't ask questions, bring some up. Seeing a pregnant woman in a store is an excellent opportunity. By the time your child is five, he should know the basic parts of his sex organs and that a baby grows in the uterus and comes out a special opening between mother's legs with the doctor's help. Be careful of terms such as, "the baby grows in Mommy's stomach" instead of "uterus"; for when a child sees his mother with the flu, he may be fearful she will vomit the baby. The term "planting a seed" to a child means putting a seed in the ground and covering it with dirt. "Daddy's penis fits into mother's vagina and the sperm joins the egg and a new life begins," is a correct way to use terms for a 6 year-old. You can draw a picture or use one of the many excellent books written for children.

By 9 years of age, girls need to know about menstruation and care of their body. Some girls begin their periods at that time. Boys need to know about wet dreams. Every child has a right to know how their body functions. There is no justification for a girl to begin to bleed and not know what is happening to her body. We can't leave that to chance.

Teenagers may have all the "facts of life," but their sex education is far from complete. They need help with emotions and feelings and want to learn about moodiness, love, venereal diseases, birth control and marriage. Help your teenager learn the emotional differences between boys and girls and that boys do get "turned on" quicker than girls, that girls enjoy sex as much as boys and that there is responsibility with sex. Girls do have sex because of love. Boys have sex, then begin to love. This is God's plan to keep sex and love together.

As a parent, know the different diseases that can be contacted sexually. Your public health department will help you with this. Be sure your child knows about venereal disease. Junior high is not too early to discuss this topic.

Teach your child how to respond warmly to strangers and yet with caution. Most sexual molesting occurs by someone the child knows. Tell your child that parts of his body are private and no one needs to touch them. If someone does, tell him to come to you and let you know. Never scold the child for this. If he feels that he will be punished, he may be frightened and not come to you. Help your older child have confidence by learning some self-defense tactics. Many communities offer courses on self defense. Nothing builds confidence more than being able to protect yourself.

Teach your child to come to you for information. What you talk about in your family is private. You are building a trust relationship when your child knows that what he asks or tells you remains in the family.

Through your example of living, children can learn that sex and love are wedded for a long lasting, satisfying relationship. Sex alone is shallow and soon loses its flavor. Sex and love combined climax the fulfillment of two people in a long-lasting relationship.

Values are that which we rate highly or cherish. They become an important part of forming our sexuality. Before a child can form a value, he must be able to reason. He needs to choose from alternatives and learn to make decisions. This takes training. His choice must be freely made and lastly, he must act on his value with a repeated pattern. This cannot possibly happen until the child is about 9 or 10 years old.

Values differ among people, but the way they are formed is the same for everyone. Piaget tells us there are stages that children grow through toward making more mature ways of making moral judgments—deciding what is right or wrong—that lead to developing values.

Up to age 7, children are developing control over their bodies. They do not understand abstract concepts, but rather understand black and white. They know right from wrong by pleasing parents and teachers.

Nine and ten year olds see intentions. They can say "I didn't mean to hurt you." At 11 and 12 years of age they are concerned with being fair. Whoever spilled the milk has to clean it up, even if the person is a very young child. At 13 and 14 years of age, the child can understand being asked to clean up the mess if his brother is too young to do so.

Dr. Lawrence Kohlberg tells us that there are six stages of moral development that adolescents and adults can be in.

In stage one, morality is developed because of fear of punishment. In this level of morality, wrong will be determined if the result will be in the form of a punishment such as a spanking, going to jail, or being fined. Expecting something in return, constitutes stage two. I will do something for you, if you will do something for me. Recognition is prized more than material reward in stage three. It is right if a person is recognized as "good." We find loyalties to groups here. Stage four constitutes right and wrong, determined by one's own duties to those in authority, such as law and order. Most adults are at this level of morality. Right and wrong in stage five are based on recognizing individual rights within the framework of *agreed* laws such as the United States Constitution. Individuals recognize that laws are made to protect rights and freedom. In stage six, right and wrong are determined by personal judgment based on self-chosen moral principals that are consistent, understandable and applied to all human beings. Here a person will stand up for his philosophy, even if there is risk to his life. Very few adults reach this stage of morality.

Parents can help their children develop morality and form values that will be a vital part of their sexuality. Before this can be done, parents must know what their own sexual values are. Part of forming a value is the repeated action of living that value. You cannot teach values unless you are living your values. It is much more difficult to teach your child not to have premarital sex, if you believe extra-marital affairs are all right and practice this.

It is important to realize that there is a difference between rules such as keeping a room clean and morality such as honesty. If a chore is not done, a discipline procedure needs to be used to teach. This does not mean the child is not moral.

Let your children participate in family decisions. Regular family get-togethers to discuss chores and rules, and family meetings, will help your child to formulate values as he listens to and observes his parents living their values.

When disciplining, do not use moralistic approaches. "You told me you would clean up this room. You're a liar," instead of "Since this room is not cleaned up, you know the consequences. You may not go out with Bobby until you are finished." Use one of the discipline procedures we have discussed earlier in the book. These methods teach. When using a consequence, be sure it relates to the incident if possible. If a child steals an object, he needs to make restitution by returning it, if possible, or by working to pay the debt. This is more effective than taking away television viewing.

Listen to, and observe your child to be aware of why he is making the moral judgment he is. Help him to see the advantages and disadvantages of his decision. Remember he must assume the responsibility for his decision. When mistakes are made, treat your child as a person. When a glass is broken, teach him to clean it up. A young child can help to clean up a mess. Apologize to your child when you are wrong. This will help your child see that adults make mistakes, too, and that we learn from our mistakes.

Provide models for your child that live the values you are teaching. Expose the child to friends, acquaintances and relatives living similar values.

As a parent you have a right to your value system. While a child is living with you he needs to respect your values. When your teenager's values differ from yours, you have a right to keep yours, if you so wish. Be ready to explain your values. It is not enough to say "because" when your teenager pushes you into a corner on a belief. Tell him why. Perhaps this is what he is looking for, to stand up against his peers. He needs ammunition and you are not giving it to him if you say "because."

Discuss controversial subjects, such as premarital sex, abortion, homosexuality, contraceptives, venereal disease, and teenage pregnancies. Get facts from professionals and give them to your child. Discuss why you believe as you do. Respect his questioning. Give him time to form his opinions.

When your teenager's values differ from yours, do not shut off communication. Tell him you disapprove of the action, not him. Remember, some values change with maturity. What you thought was most important ten years ago may not be so today.

In the area of sexuality, your teenager is bombarded with "right" and "wrong" based on value systems that differ from person to person. He must formulate his own value system by adulthood. Your stability and example of morality and values will form the foundation on which his values will be made. He may move away from you, but with communication and warmth, he can return, bringing joy to you as a parent.

SEXUALITY

Buzz Questions

1. What are your early recollections of sex education? How did you learn about sex? Did you feel adequately prepared?

2. Would you teach your child sex education the same way you learned? Explain.

3. What are questions that preschoolers ask? Elementary school aged children? Teenagers? Who should answer them, father or mother, or both?

4. "Boys don't cry." "Little girls are neat and clean." List other differences between the sexes that we make with our children, stereotyping them into roles.

SEXUALITY

Sexuality involves the whole self of male or female. This includes teaching our children "the facts of life," helping them form relationships with the same sex and with the opposite sex, teaching them to respect and enjoy their bodies so they can respect and enjoy others, and helping them to form values.

WHAT PARENTS CAN DO TO TEACH SEXUALITY TO THEIR CHILDREN:

1. Help children become familiar with their bodies by giving appropriate information at the right ages. Every person has a right to know their body functions.

2. Teach children to respect and love their bodies so they can love and respect others.

3. Help them develop a positive self-image so they can feel good about themselves.

4. Satisfy their curiosity about the opposite sex. (If you have all boys, babysit a baby girl).

5. Give correct information, not "old wives' tales."

6. Train your child to come to you for information.

7. Know the venereal diseases, how they can be contracted and their dangers.

8. Teach your child how to respond warmly to strangers, yet with caution.

9. The example of a happy marriage is an excellent teacher of sexuality.

10. Teach your child that sex and love go together for a long-lasting relationship.

11. Provide good reading material to your child, be aware of and help plan school programs teaching sex education, and help your teenagers locate supervised groups that teach sexuality.

12. Help teenagers develop interests and hobbies so they can handle their sexual feelings without having them dominate their lives.

SEXUALITY

Sex Education

Many people think of sex education as a task, and they refer to "the parents' job," or the "job of the school." Actually sex education is the parents' privilege, for they have the privilege of sharing daily life with their children, cherishing them and guiding them in many of the early experiences that can make sex education *sound* education.

General Principles to Remember

1. Sex education begins at birth. Cuddling, holding, and touching are teaching your child sexuality.

2. Teach your child the parts of the body by using the correct words, such as penis, vagina, uterus, testicles, urine, bowel movements, etc.

3. Both parents can answer questions. By puberty, girls will probably ask their mothers more questions, while boys will more frequently question their fathers.

4. Be sure to answer questions truthfully. If you don't know an answer, look it up. Books from the library will be helpful. Your health department is happy to help you with information.

5. Know what the child is asking and answer simply. A question like "What do you think it means?" will help you know where his understanding is.

6. Children will ask questions over and over.

7. Try to answer questions with as little emotion as possible.

8. Pay attention to attitudes. Be sure your attitudes have been thought about carefully and are logical.

9. By school age, the child should know in simple terms the main parts of his sex organs, where babies come from, how babies get started, and how they are born.

10. Books and pictures make good teachers. Be sure the book is appropriate for the age level.

11. When explaining processes such as intercourse, stay away from terms like "planting seeds." Children think concretely and will visualize a garden being planted.

12. By the time children are nine years of age they should know all the parts of their body, mating, how a baby is developed and born, and functions such as menstruation and the release of sperm.

13. Teenagers will know most basic facts of sex education, but need help with emotional feelings of sexuality and value formation. Some questions they will have might be:
    ● What is homosexual, bisexual, heterosexual?
    ● How will I know when I'm in love?
    ● What kinds of contraceptives are there? Are they dangerous?
    ● Can I get VD from toilet seats?
    ● What will you do if I get pregnant?

SEXUALITY

How Would You Answer?

All of the following true and false statements came from the mouths of junior high boys and girls. In the space to the right of each statement, mark under the true column if true, the false column to indicate a false statement.

	TRUE	FALSE
1. Some homosexual behavior is a normal part of growing up.	_____	_____
2. Something is wrong with the male who has one testicle lower than the other.	_____	_____
3. Saran Wrap and Cokes are effective contraceptives.	_____	_____
4. A girl as young as 5 years and a woman as old as 57 years have given birth to children.	_____	_____
5. Humans and lower animals cannot crossbreed.	_____	_____
6. Douching is one of the adequate and satisfactory methods of contraception.	_____	_____
7. Sexual intercourse is habit forming.	_____	_____
8. A girl is safe from pregnancy if sexual intercourse occurs during menstruation.	_____	_____
9. Alcohol often causes temporary impotence.	_____	_____
10. Masturbation causes certain types of emotional and mental problems.	_____	_____
11. If a girl does not have a maidenhead (hymen) it is good proof that she is not a virgin.	_____	_____
12. Homosexuals can ordinarily be identified by certain distinctive mannerisms or physical characteristics.	_____	_____
13. A boy has to masturbate before he can get his penis small again.	_____	_____

14. Babies are deformed when a couple has incorrect intercourse. _____ _____
15. Doctors can tell if you have been masturbating. _____ _____
16. The size of the penis determines the amount of sexual pleasure. _____ _____
17. Girls are very fragile during menstruation. _____ _____
18. When girls have milk in their breast it is safe to have intercourse. _____ _____
19. To be popular with the boys it is necessary for a girl to have intercourse. _____ _____
20. It is dangerous for a girl to take part in sports, to take a bath, or to shampoo her hair during menstruation. _____ _____
21. Certain foods are valuable in increasing the sex drive.

_____ _____

MORALITY

Values differ among people; but the formation of morality, right and wrong leading to forming values, is the same for everyone.

Dr. Lawrence Kohlberg, Harvard psychologist who has extended Piaget's psychology of moral development to adult growth, names six stages of moral development. Most adults never reach stages five and six.

1. Right and wrong are determined by fear of punishment.

2. Expecting something in return causes some people to decide what is right and wrong.

3. Recognition is more valuable than material reward in stage three of moral development.

4. Morality is determined by one's duties to those in authority, law and order. Most adults are at this level of moral judgment.

5. Right and wrong are determined by recognizing individual rights based on agreed laws, such as the U.S. Constitution.

6. Moral principals are self-chosen by personal judgment and are consistent, understandable and applied to all persons. A person at this level of morality will stand up for his beliefs, even if the outcome is death.

What stage of moral development are you in? What values have you derived from your stage in moral development? Are these the same goals you hope your child will achieve? Why or why not?

SEXUALITY

Values

Values are that which we cherish, consider or rate highly. It is important that we know what our values are through value clarification. Parents have a right to their values and need to let their children know what they are. Your example of living is the best teacher of values. Before a value can be formed:

- A child must be able to reason.

- He must be able to make decisions.

- A choice must be made from alternatives.

- There needs to be a repeated pattern of behavior which shows rational choice.

- The choice must be freely made. "I am doing this because I want to, not because I am forced to."

When children's values do not agree with yours:

- Listen to what they are saying. They may purposely take an opposite stand to learn why you believe as you do. They may need this information for defense with their peer group. "Because I said so," is not a valid answer.

- Explain why you believe as you do.

- While a child is living with you, he needs to respect your values.

- After the age of emancipation, your child has a right to live his own values, accepting the consequences.

- Try not to shut off communication if your child suffers a consequence from his action. He will need you more than ever. He needs to know you do not approve of his action but you still care for him.

- Values change with maturity. Your continued stability and example of your values will help him mature.

A DIFFERENCE IN VALUES

Number the following situations 1 through 5 in order of your tolerance in dealing with them. Number 1 will be the least tolerable, number 2 the next, etc. with number 5 being the most tolerable to you.

_____Your 4 year old son masturbates in the grocery store.

_____Your 5 year old has his pants pulled down and is "playing doctor" with a neighborhood girl when you walk in the room.

_____Your 8 year old comes home with the F-4 letter word.

_____Your 14 year old comes home after his curfew of 11:00 P.M. repeatedly.

_____Your 15 year old daughter wants you to get the pill for her.

SEXUALITY

Observation Sheet

1. What questions are your children asking about sex?

2. How are you answering them?

3. List specific ways you are helping your child develop his or her maleness or femaleness?

4. What ways do you observe your child interacting sexually in his peer group? (Talking, dressing, body language, etc.)

5. What sexual values do you see your child forming? Do they agree or disagree with yours?

TEN COMMANDMENTS OF PARENTING

1. Enjoy your children. Being a parent is a privilege. Children grow so quickly and leave home so soon.

2. Understand your children. Learn what concepts they are capable of at their age. Help them grow in all areas of development; intellectually, emotionally, socially, physically, sexually and spiritually. Then your teaching will be effective and learning long lasting.

3. Communicate with your children. Words are threads with which we are woven together.

4. Discipline your children. Teach them to be sociably acceptable and self-disciplined in a way that will not lower their self-image.

5. Help your children understand they are made up of emotions and feelings and are sexual beings. We are not responsible for feelings, but for the consequences of our feelings.

6. Develop a long lasting and good relationship with your child. Then all your strengths and weaknesses as a parent can be tolerated by him.

7. Teach your children to feel good about themselves so they can feel good about others.

8. Give your children moral guidance so they can grow into adults who care about others.

9. Love your children for what and who they are. They are individuals entrusted into your care. You have been chosen from all parents to parent the child you have.

10. Learn parenting skills so you can feel confident as a parent, and your responsibility as a parent can be made joyous.

NOTES

*Joy and sorrow are inseparable,
the deeper the sorrow the greater the
joy that can be experienced*

SPIRITUALITY, DEVELOPING RELIGIOUS VALUES

SPIRITUALITY—DEVELOPING RELIGIOUS VALUES

"A living faith is always on trial, we call it faith for that reason."
J. Edgar Park

Spirituality is the breath of life we receive as a gift from God. It so encompasses us that it is the intercourse of body and soul. The product of this intercourse being an awareness of the existence of a supreme being. This awareness causes us to practice religion, the service and adoration of God. The way we practice religion is determined by the religious values we have formed.

The steps we learned in forming values are applicable in forming religious values. There must be the ability to reason, which presupposes a certain age. The skill of making decisions is necessary, as a choice needs to be made from alternatives. This choice must be freely made, and there needs to be a repeated pattern of behavior. The value needs to be lived.

The attitudes and values our parents had are very influential in how we feel about religion. Most of our religious formation began very early in life. Children learn about God through their relationship with their parents. Studies have shown the father image plays an important role in how the child will view God. A strict, unbending, oftentimes cross parent will influence a child's interpretation of God as a strict disciplinarian. A patient, loving, open parent will present an entirely different image to the child and so his image of God will relate to this type of parent. Punishment which uses God as fear, "God is watching over you, he knows everything you do. I can't see you but he can." develops a fearful image of God that can be carried for a lifetime unless it is changed somewhere along life's path.

People we have come in contact with also have helped us to form our religious values. Teachers, clergy, relatives and peers influenced us by what they said or did or what they did not say or do. Silence teaches. The church's teaching of religion is passed on to us through people.

Crises we have had in our lives determine what religious values we have. Crisis can temper us or bring out bitterness. How we have interpreted God's part in the crisis, or the "self talk" we have experienced, determines how we react to Him through religion.

Cultural background and tradition pass down customs about religion that become part of us. Ways of practicing religion, rituals, and ceremonies are part of tradition.

Formal education of the church's teachings plays an important role in developing our religious values. If experiences were pleasant, we have comfortable memories of learning about God. If our questions were answered and we were given time, love and patience, we feel good about our religion. If we were put down, told things that did not make sense, or were not listened to, negative attitudes affected our value making.

Society, in general, has influenced us. Books, media, social norms and research are influential in our thinking. As we learn more about people and how they interrelate we learn more about ourselves and how we relate to God.

It is important that we determine what our religious values are if we are to teach religion to our children. This takes effort and necessitates taking time to be alone to understand why we believe as we do.

To give you an idea of your value system, try the following values clarification. Number, in order of importance to you, the following:

- Your teenager missed Sunday worship,
- He is failing a subject in school,
- Your teenager has no tolerance for minority groups.

What you choose as being most important will tell you about your values. Forcing a teenager to attend Mass may "turn him off" to worship. Try to discuss the "why" of his not wanting to go. Work from there. He may feel he does not fit in. Church is for adults. Perhaps it has no meaning for him at this time in his life. Your teenager may see contradictions among the people at worship. Adults go to church each Sunday and yet take part in shady business deals or are not helpful to others. He may feel he needs the freedom to decide whether to go or not, and yet he may feel he is not mature enough to make this decision. Encourage him and set an example for him to follow.

Failing a subject in school needs attention but should not be a primary value. Christians care about each other. The third statement should be of concern to you in teaching religious values.

It is easy to use the church as a crutch. "This is what the church teaches so you have to believe it." Your teenager wants to know what it is you are teaching. Why do you believe what the church is teaching? Take time to write down what you feel are the most important goals of your religion. Can you explain each one? What has convinced you of its importance? Look at each goal again. Pick one. What values have you made for yourself from this goal? Are you living these values? Using this same goal, decide how you would go about teaching this area to your child.

A goal of Christianity you might choose is, "Love Thy Neighbor." From this goal, values you may have made for yourself are, "Treat others with respect, actively listen to others when they talk to you, and help others when you are able to." The next step is to live these values, not only with "neighbors" but with your children. Respect your child. Knock on closed doors before entering, listen to what he has to tell you without being judgmental and show him easier ways to do things. These are ways you can teach this value to your child.

Teaching your child about love will establish a warm, caring relationship between both of you. This, in turn, will help him form a loving relationship with God. Share your love with your child.

How will you know you have a warm, caring relationship with your child? Body contact is a good sign. A hug, or kiss, or holding hands are positive signs. When your child talks to you about happenings, or tells you his feelings, he is confiding in you. Can you remember how good you felt when your child did something for you without being asked? How about when he told you he understood just how you were feeling and tried to help make things right again? These are all signs of a good relationship.

When you feel you are often angry with your child; if your child isolates himself in his room for hours at a time; if yelling is a way of life in your family; if small problems blow up out of proportion; or, if sarcasm is used more often than you like, then you will know your relationship needs improving.

Fulfilling your child's needs will help him feel good about himself. If he feels good about himself, he will feel good about others. His self-esteem will carry over to how he feels about God.

Your child needs affection. He needs to be touched, to be hugged or kissed. A teenager who is easily embarrassed by signs of affection will know you care if you straighten his shirt or pat him on the back. He needs your body language to tell him he is lovable.

Praise your child when he accomplishes a feat or when he pleases you. Your smile, nod or words of encouragement make him feel good and will be the incentive he needs to try again.

Respect his privacy. Knock on a closed door. Help him to have time alone. Show him all the consideration you would an adult. This will make him feel important.

Respect your child's friendship. Let your house be open to his friends. Remember your home is his home too. Never embarrass him in front of his peers. Make rules regarding visits with him, and take disciplinary actions when he is alone. Be friendly and talk with his friends, but respect their privacy.

Listen to your child. He needs someone to talk to. He needs to feel that no matter what he talks about, you will feel it is important. Whatever happens out in the world, he has someone who will listen and who cares for him.

Fulfilling needs of your child will help him to form his relationship to God. He will be learning to love God, to respect Him, to form a friendship with Him and to talk to Him. Through your family, your child is learning to be part of a spiritual family.

Teach your child all about life, the painful experiences as well as the pleasant ones. Help him to see there is sorrow in life; without experiencing sorrow, we cannot fully experience joy.

When your child's pet dies, don't hide it from him or replace it with a new one without letting him know. Talk about it. Let him grieve for his pet. Funerals and burial services are for the living, to help them come to grips with what has happened.

If your child has been looking forward to a party and making plans for weeks to attend, he will be very disappointed when, on the morning of the party, he wakes up sick. Be supportive, but let him experience that disappointment.

When a joyful event occurs, celebrate. A special dinner, a cake, eating out, or even a card to express your feelings, will help him experience joy to its fullest. This is learning about life and learning about life is learning about God and forming religious values.

Make memories for your children. What will your children remember about you when they are grown? Will they remember the time your family shared together, or will they remember only doing daily chores? Will they remember vacations, places and people they met? What will they remember about how you talked, dressed, smelled, laughed, cried? Will they remember you as cross, yelling and nagging, or will they remember that you smiled often and went out of your way to plan excitement for the family?

How does your family celebrate? What do you do for birthdays, holidays and special occasions? Do you plan something special or are these just ordinary days? Celebrations take the ordinary out of life and add sparkle to living.

Religiously, how do you celebrate? October and May are beautiful months to make an altar for Mary. Celebrate feast days. Baptismal anniversaries are a reason for celebration. Family camps are a yearly event for the whole family to look forward to. A family prayer at mealtime can make memories if each can participate.

Think back for a moment to the home you grew up in. What memories about it were pleasant? Which ones unpleasant? What was your favorite room? Why? Can you remember colors, smells, furniture arrangements?

Try to make your home a pleasant and happy place. Flowers are a "thing of beauty." Use them. Baking creates wonderful smells. Building home projects together creates memories. Keep your home in order. Decorate your home together. Your home should express your family's personality.

Making memories is helping your child feel good about life. If he feels good about life, he will feel good about God, who created life.

What part does prayer play in your life? Prayer is an important part of religion. Teach your child to talk to God. Before meals is an excellent time to talk to God. Let each member of the family have a turn during the week. We should not only ask God for things, but thank Him as well. Ask for His blessings. Tell God your trials and joys of the day and ask for His guidance. Let him know how you are feeling and why. God needs to be talked about and to, in your home so children can learn He is a real part of your family.

Teaching the Bible is most effective if it is interpreted into present day living. To teach religious values from the Bible, take the stories that are most exciting first. Talk about how the people lived during that period of time and discuss what was important to them. Then take the story and apply it to your family. What does it mean today?

Find a teaching in the New Testament that teaches the same concept that a story in the Old Testament does. How was it meaningful to the people in the Old Testament, in Christ's time? Then discuss how it is meaningful today. The readings from each Sunday Mass can serve as a guide for your family. Take these readings and make them applicable to the teenager's life. Without doing this, the readings will have no meaning to him.

Teenagers are testers. They will test and evaluate while they are sorting information together to form their own values. Teenagers will look for support from their parents. They expect us to be on their side and to show concern. Even though it is not always possible to agree with what your teenager is doing, you need to tell him why you disagree in a way that tells him he is still wanted and loved. Talk about the action, not him.

Your teenager wants you to lead him from childhood to adulthood. He needs to know that you will help him to emancipate himself, that you will give him support and help so he can become a responsible, self-disciplined and lovable person who can make decisions for himself. From the time he was born, you were preparing him to leave you, and building a long-lasting, loving relationship.

He needs discipline to learn what is socially acceptable and what is not. He wants and needs rules that are fair and not overbearing. He wants to be part of making those rules.

Your teenager wants to respect and trust you, and in turn wants you to respect and trust him. He wants to be given responsibility to prove himself and along with that proven responsibility he wants privileges.

It is important for your teenagers to know that you are stable, that you will not change your mind easily, that you have principles, that you know why you have those principles and that you stand by them.

Your teenager needs outlets for his energy. He needs activities and places to go. Even though he will be away from home more than ever, home is still a very important place for him. It is there as security, a place of stability for him.

He needs his peers. They are an integral part of his developing into an adult. He wants you to recognize this. He wants you to know that he is sensitive and needs others besides his family. He is sympathetic and very protective of his friends. They are important to him. They help him to feel lovable and worthwhile.

Teenagers will form religious values by learning religion as it is applicable to everyday living. This begins in families. The true meaning of religion is how we live our lives, by example and helping others. Being Christian does not only mean working in church-oriented activities. A father who has worked all day and comes home and wants to read the newspaper is being Christian. A mother who is exhausted at the end of the day after caring for her family is no less Christian than a woman working on the church bazaar. A child can live Christianity by attending school and his activities. We have been programmed into a stereotyped, Christian individual. We need to help our children see that Christians come in all forms, shapes and occupations and that we live our religion as we interact with those around us.

Sometimes, no matter how we have tried, our teenagers will not see religion as we do. What can you do when your child's values in religion are in opposition to yours?

First of all, be yourself. Do not pretend to live one set of values while you live another. Be honest with your teenager. Let him know your feelings. Be sure he knows what your beliefs are and why.

Study your faith. Read about it. Attend discussion groups and classes offered by your church. The more you know, the more you can strengthen your faith. Talk with others who share your beliefs. Study controversial issues. Know what is happening and being discussed in the world.

Clarify what your religious values are and be sure you are living them. This is the best example of religion you can give your teenagers.

Express your values in a non-authoritarian manner. Talk about your values. Don't lecture. Try to counsel and listen to your teenager. Do not use threats and punishments. They are not effective in value formation.

When your teenager comes to you with a question, listen carefully to what he is asking. Respond with your feelings and then answer the question. Stay away from "because I said so." This will not give your teenager the ammunition he needs to form his values.

One parent told me that his sixteen year-old boy questioned him antagonistically about abortion, seemingly wanting a multitude of reasons why his father believed as he did. The father gave as many reasons as he could and remained puzzled by this overly eager questioning. Two weeks later he discovered why his son had been so eager for the discussion on abortion. While talking with his son's peer group, he learned that his boy had held his own in a peer group discussion on abortion, using many of the arguments his father had given him. His son had ammunition to defend his newly formed value.

My fourteen year-old daughter came home from school with the question, "What would you do if I were pregnant?" Carefully holding on to the dish I was drying, I was silent for a few seconds, gathering thoughts together. "Why is she asking this? Good God, is she pregnant? What do we do if she is?" Questions tumbled through my mind in my "self-talk." Then calmly I told my daughter my feelings. "I'd be hurt and disappointed. Then I might feel angry and probably sad, thinking of you and your future." Then I added, "But you are my daughter and I'll always love and help you." Those were the magic words she wanted to hear. She wanted to know if I would still love her if she had this problem. We talked for about an hour and I learned that a girl she had heard about had gotten pregnant and was "disowned" by her parents. This had upset my daughter more than the pregnancy itself. Try to figure out why your child is asking his question. Take time to listen and keep communication open.

Do not criticize your child for expressing his views. Try not to be judgmental. Listen, then offer your views. Let him know that he has to make the final decision on his values, but that he also has to accept the responsibilities and consequences that go along with that value.

Stay away from a moralizing, "I'm right and you are wrong," approach. This approach puts your child on the defensive and he will fight against you even if he believes as you do. He'll want to prove he is right.

Be aware of what your church is offering teenagers for social activities and what they are doing to help them learn about their faith. Invite him to attend functions. Encourage him to bring a friend so he will feel more comfortable. Offer transportation or form car pools. Your teenager needs to be in a peer group. Learning will be more effective with interactions of peers and a trained leader, than with you as a parent during this stage of his value formation.

Expose your child to models who believe as you do. Adult friends and acquaintances can serve as models. Autobiographies to read will provide examples of value living. Discussions with teenagers who have similar values will provide stimulation. Ideally, schools teaching similar values will foster a value-formation atmosphere and help the parent teach his values. This is what the ghetto provided for youth. Family, schools, churches and community all taught the same values. Similar values were formed easily. Today this is not so. Values are formed from many choices and are more difficult to formulate.

Your teenager wants religion to be a present day living experience. Make religious experiences a part of your living experience. Take a community issue and discuss what your family can do to help. Any area of living is a religious area. They cannot be separated. The problem of fuel conservation is of concern to all of us. What can your family do to conserve fuel? You might discuss forming a car pool and making less trips to the store. Lowering your thermostat and using less hot water are alternatives that might be mentioned. Help your teenager see that this is concern for others by trying to live together and help each other in this world. God's commandment again is evident, "Love Thy Neighbor." This is religion.

Read the newspaper and discuss current events. Relate them to religion. Show your child how religion is a way of life, not something you only do on Sunday.

Be open to controversial discussions. Topics such as birth control, abortion, pre-marital sex and homosexuality are of interest to teenagers and should be to you also. What are both sides to the picture? How do you feel about each issue and why? Discuss the pros and cons. Let your child know he can discuss any topic with you. If you don't know information on a topic, look it up or have someone help you with it. Admit to your teenager that you need more information. Ask him to help. Learn together.

Lastly, do no be overanxious. Do what you can in teaching religious values. Keep communication open between you and your teenager. Remember, your teenager is an individual and has to form his own value system. Have faith in God's creation. No matter how far he may wander from your value system, act in a loving, supportive manner, as you live your own values for example. Plant the seeds, life will water them, and God will make them grow. This is Joy in Parenting.

BUZZ SESSION

1. What are your early recollections of the religious education you had?

2. Do you feel positive or negative about these recollections?

3. Who was the most influential in the formation of your religious values? Your father, your mother, or another person?

4. What part did teachers play in forming your values? Your peers?

5. Would you teach your child religious values differently than you learned? Why or why not?

SPIRITUALITY—YOUR RELIGIOUS VALUES

In order to help our children form religious values, we must be aware of what our religious values are.

1. What do you feel is the ultimate goal of religion?

2. Do you view religion as a part of every day living?

3. What goals have you set for yourself to grow spiritually?

4. What is your image of God?

5. List words that you feel describe God.

6. What concept do you have of heaven? Of hell?

7. What role does attending church play in your life?

8. What basic religious attitudes do you have?

9. Are these attitudes those you want your children to have?

10. What does teaching religion mean to you as a parent?

11. Who should teach religious values to your child?

12. How early do you feel religious education should begin?

MEMORIES

Memories are an important part of our lives. What we have seen, heard, tasted, smelled or touched becomes part of us and forms either pleasant or unpleasant memories. Your child's feelings about God and religion will be influenced by the memories he has of his family.

1. What do you think will be the fondest memories your children will have of you?

2. What could you do to build more pleasurable memories for your children?

3. How will these memories relate to the image your child will have of God?

WHAT TO DO WHEN YOUR TEENAGER'S RELIGIOUS VALUES DIFFER FROM YOURS

1. Study and know your faith.

2. Know what your religious values are.

3. Live your religious values.

4. Be yourself. Do not play a role. Your child will see through this.

5. Express your values to your teenager in a non-authoritarian manner.

6. Do not answer his questions with, "because." Give him a reason for your belief so he will have ammunition to form his value system.

7. Be a listener and a counselor. Don't lecture.

8. Do not criticize your child for expressing his views.

9. Stay away from a moralizing "I am right, you are wrong" approach. That will just make your teenager negative.

10. Invite your child to learn what your church teaches.

11. Provide opportunities for him to interact with a peer group in a church setting.

12. Expose your child to other models who believe as you do.

13. Make religion a part of your living experience. Your teenager wants to feel religion is in the present, not in the past.

14. Relate current events to religion.

15. Be open to controversial discussions on birth control, abortion, homosexuality and pre-marital sex.

16. Do not be over-anxious. Do what you can. Remember, your teenager has to form his own value system.

OBSERVATION SHEET

Religious values are best taught to your child if you are living your values. Your beliefs, words and actions need to coincide for effective teaching. You are teaching your child religious values even if you are silent.

1. What kinds of questions is your child asking about God?

2. Listen and record a conversation your child has with God. Is his way of praying the same as yours?

3. List as many ways as possible that your home expresses your religious values.

4. What religious attitudes and behavior do you express to your child?

5. List words that your child expresses about his experiences in church.

PRAYER FOR PARENTS

"Oh, God, make me a better parent.

Help me to understand my children, to listen patiently to what they have to say and to respond to their questions kindly.

Keep me from interrupting them, talking back to them and contradicting them.

Make me as courteous to them as I would have them be to me.

Give me the courage to confess my sins against my children and ask them for forgiveness when I know I have done wrong.

May I not vainly hurt the feelings of my children.

Forbid that I should laugh at their mistakes, or to resort to shame and ridicule as punishment.

Let me not tempt a child to lie or steal.

Guide me hour by hour that I may demonstrate by all I say and do that honesty produces happiness.

Reduce, I pray, the meanness in me. May I cease to nag; and when I am out of sorts, help me, O Lord, to hold my tongue.

Blind me to the little errors of my children and help me to see the good things they do.

Give me a ready word for honest praise.

Help me treat my children as those of their own age.

Let me not expect from them the judgment of adults.

Allow me not to rob them of the opportunity to wait upon themselves, to think, to choose and to make their own decisions.

Forbid that I should ever punish them for my selfish satisfaction.

May I grant them all their wishes that are reasonable and have the courage always to withhold a privilege which I know will do them harm.

Make me so fair and just, so considerate and companionable that they will have genuine esteem for me.

Let me be loved and imitated by my children.

Oh, God, do give me calm and poise, and self-control.

Ann Landers

NOTES

PARENTING BIBLIOGRAPHY

PARENTING MATERIALS: Books, Pamphets, Films and Cassettes.

Parenting in 1976: A Listing From Parenting Materials Information Center.
Early Childhood Division, Southwest Educational Development Laboratory,
211 East 7th Street, Austin, Texas 78701.
An up-to-date list of parenting materials divided into 19 major subject areas. A
complete publisher's list with mailing addresses included.

SELF-ESTEEM

James, Muriel & Jongeward, Dorothy. *Born to Win.* Reading, Massachusetts:
Addison-Wesley, 1971.
An adult Transactional Analysis approach to self esteem. Exercises at the end
of each chapter to help you better know yourself.

Briggs, Dorothy. *Your Child's Self Esteem.* Garden City, New York: Doubleday,
1970.
This book explains specifically how high self-esteem can be built in children
of all ages.

Felker, Donald. *Building Positive Self-Concepts.* Minneapolis, Minnesota:
Burgess, 1974.
Explains ways to develop a positive self-image in children. Encourages parents to teach children to evaluate their own actions.

Canfield, Jack & Wells, Harold. *100 Ways to Enchance Self-Concept in the
Classroom.* Englewood Cliffs, New Jersey: Prentice-Hall Inc., 1976.
A handbook for teachers and parents. Easy-to-read and follow practical ways
to enhance self-concept in youth.

COMMUNICATION

Ginott, Haim. *Between Parent and Teenager.* New York: Macmillan Co., 1969.
Excellent on establishing communication between parent and teenager.

Gordon, Thomas. *Parent Effectiveness Training.* New York: Peter H. Wyden,
Inc., 1970.

Active listening is an approach used for better communication between parent and child. The "I-You" statements are explained. As a discipline procedure, the "No Win-No Lose" method is discussed.

Satir, Virginia. *Peoplemaking.* Palo Alto, California: Science & Behavior Books, Inc., 1972.
Family communication is discussed in depth, with exercises to follow.

Harris, Thomas. *I'm OK, You're OK: A Practical Guide to Transactional Analysis.* New York: Harper & Row, 1969.
A complete discussion of our three ego states: parent, child and adult; also discusses how they function when we interact with others.

Bienvenu, Hillard. *Parent-Teenager Communication.* Public Affairs Pamphlets, 381 Park Avenue South, New York, New York, 1969.
Explicit steps to help parents communicate with their teenagers.

AGES AND STAGES

Fraiberg, Selma. *Magic Years.* New York: Scribner's, Charles, Sons, 1968.
Excellent suggestions on helping your young child build a healthy conscience.

Ilg, Frances & Ames, Louise. *Child Behavior.* New York: Harper and Row, 1972.
This book is organized by topics covering physical, intellectual, emotional and social growth stages of children up to age 10.

Dittmann, Laura. *Your Child From 1 to 6.* U. S. Department of Health, Education and Welfare. Washington, D.C., 1975.
Basic child development with emphasis on physical development.

Stone, L. Josephy & Church, Joseph. *Childhood and Adolescence, A Psychology of the Growing Person.* New York: Random House, Inc., 1975.
A well-written textbook on child development from birth to adulthood. Knowledgeable information on middle childhood and adolescence.

Sheehy, Gail. *Passages.* New York: Dutton, E. P., & Co., Inc., 1976.
Excellent book on adult stages of growth.

Lowenfeld, Viktor. *Creative and Mental Growth.* New York: Macmillan Co., 1975.
Helps parents and teachers understand the mental and emotional development of children through their art work.

DISCIPLINE

Dreikurs, Rudolf & Soltz, Vicki. *Children: The Challenge.* New York: Hawthorne Books, Inc., 1964.
Natural and logical consequences are discussed as an appraoch to discipline. How to handle power struggles, along with an explanation of new approaches to discipline in democratic society, as opposed to an autocratic society.

Dreikurs, Rudolf. *A Parents' Guide to Child Discipline.* New York: Hawthorne Books, Inc., 1970.
A concentrated effort of natural and logical consequences as an approach to discipline.

Dodson, Fitzhugh. *How to Parent.* New York: Nash Publishing Corporation, 1970.
Parenting skills for parents of young children.

Ginott, Haim. *Between Parent and Child.* New York: Macmillan Publishing Co., Inc., 1965.
Skills in parenting, basically for the child under 10. Methods of communication are discussed in relationship to discipline.

Faber, Adele & Mazlish, Elaine. *Liberated Parents —Liberated Children.* New York: Avon Books, 1975.
Parents who were students of Ginott put his teachings to practice. Successes and failures are numerated.

Patterson, Gerald. *Living With Children.* Champaign, Illinois: Research Press, 1973.
Discipline skills based on behavior modification. Reinforcers and "Time-Out" are explained as alternatives in Discipline.

Patterson, Gerald. *Families.* Champaign, Illinois: Research Press, 1975.
A more in-depth version of *Living With Children.*

Chapman, A. H. *Games Children Play.* New York: Berkley Publishing Corporation, 1972.
Classic games children manipulate their parents into playing.

Albrecht, Margaret. *Parents and Teenagers: Getting Through to Each Other.* New York: Parents Magazine Press, 1972.
Provides background and viewpoints to help teenagers and parents.

EMOTIONS AND FEELINGS

Ross Laboratories, Columbus, Ohio. *Your Child's Fears.*
A pamphlet obtained through doctor's offices. Brief, but well-done discussion on children's fears.

Shan, Eda Le. *What Makes Me Feel This Way.* New York: Collier Books, 1972.
An excellent book written for children to help them understand their feelings. Very good for parents, also.

Smith, Lynn & Clanton, Gordon. *Jealousy.* Englewood Cliffs, New Jersey: Prentice-Hall, Inc., 1976.
An in depth explanation of the history of human jealousy. Although mostly geared to marital feelings of jealousy, much can be used in parent-child and sibling relationships.

Ross Laboratories, Columbus, Ohio. *Your Children's Quarrels.*
A pamphlet obtained through doctors' offices. A brief discussion on understanding why your children quarrel and what parents can do to promote harmony among siblings.

SEXUALITY

Mayle, Peter. *Where Did I Come From?* Secaucus, New Jersey: Stuart, Lyle, Inc., 1973.
Facts of life explained for children to puberty. Illustrations delightful.

Mayle, Peter. *What's Happening To Me?* Secaucus, New Jersey: Stuart, Lyle, Inc., 1975.
Questions and answers for children from puberty on. Illustrations put parents and children at ease.

Child Study Association of America. *What to Tell Your Children About Sex.* New York: Hawthorn Books, Inc., 1968.
Questions children ask about sex and how to answer them.

Nilsson, Lennart. *How Was I Born?* New York: Delacorte Press, 1975.
A photographic story of reproduction and birth for children by a world-famous photographer.

Gordon, Sol. *Let's Make Sex a Household Word: A Guide for Parents and Teachers.* New York: John Day Co., 1975.
Skills to help parents to be the primary sex educators of their children.

Simon, Sidney & Howe, Leland & Kirschenbaum, Howard. *Values Clarification.* New York: Hart Publishing Company, 1972.
A handbook of strategies to help clarify personal values.

Duska, Ronald & Whelan, Mariellen. *Moral Development: A Guide to Piaget and Kohlberg.* New York: Paulist Press, 1975.
A good introduction to the best known moral psychologists. Advice for parents who want to teach moral education at home.

CRISIS PARENTING

Stewart, Mark & Olds, Sally. *Raising a Hyperactive Child.* New York: Harper & Row, 1973.
Parenting skills for parents who are raising a child diagnosed as hyperactive.

Gardner, Richard. *Boys and Girls Book About Divorce.* New York: Aronson, Jason, Inc., 1971.
Book written for children to help them deal with this crisis. Children's guilt feelings about their parent's divorce are handled expertly.

Grollman, Earl. *Explaining Death to Children.* Boston, Massachusetts: Beacon Press, 1969.
Group of experts discuss various approaches on the subject.

Kubler-Ross, Elisabeth. *Questions & Answers on Death and Dying.* New York: Macmillan Publishing Co., Inc., 1974.
New approaches on handling our feelings about death.

Sarason, Irwin & Linder, Karen & Crnic, Keith. *A Guide for Foster Parents.* New York: Human Sciences Press, 1976.
A complete guide including the definition of foster care, its relationship to child welfare, problems and needs of foster children, discipline involved, the teenage foster child and the relationship of the foster parent to the natural parent.

Klein, Carole. *The Single Parent Experience.* New York: Avon Books, 1973.
A book written for the single parent. Problems encountered and parenting skills are discussed.

The Exceptional Parent Magazine. Post Office Box 4944. Manchester, New Hampshire, 03108.
Gives practical guidance for parents who have handicapped children.

Rosenbaum, Jean. *Stepparenting.* Corte Madea, California: Chandler and Sharp Publications, 1977.
Help for Stepparents, a neglected area of parenting.

SPIRITUALITY

Brusselmans, Christiane. *Religion for Little Children.* Huntington, Indiana: Our Sunday Visitor Publications, 1970.
This book stresses home as "the most important classroom for religious education."

Curran, Dolores. *Who, Me Teach My Child Religion?* Minneapolis, Minnesota: Mine Publications, Inc., 1970.
A Catholic parent's viewpoint of how religion can be taught in the home.

DiGiacomo, James and Wakin, Edward. *We Were Never Their Age.* New York: Holt, Rinehart and Winston, Inc., 1972.
"This book is for parents, educators, and other concerned adults who wonder if the kids really are different, who would like to know what our young people really want, and who think the solution cannot be as simple as putting our foot down."

Larsen, Earnest and Galvin, Patricia. *Will Religion Make Sense To Your Child?* Liguori, Missouri: Liguorian Books, 1970.
The authors present new emphases in religious thinking and ideas on how to break down the material for children.

McIntyre, Marie. *Parents, You've Got a Lot to Give.* Notre Dame, Indiana: Ave Maria Press, 1972.
A series of essays to help the parent integrate Christian life by relating religion to every day living.

NOTES

JOY IN PARENTING WORKSHOPS

Available In All Areas

Classes and workshops on Joy in Parenting concepts are being held in many areas.

To reinforce the teachings of Joy in Parenting, workshops can be offered in your community for churches, schools, agencies and organizations.

Workshops are available for those interested in teaching the series of classes or for parents to help them gain further insight into the concepts of Joy in Parenting and to help them become "better" parents.

For more information with no obligation or cost write to:

JOY IN PARENTING
3713 Cherry Lane
Medford, Oregon 97501

ABOUT THE AUTHOR

Jo Schlehofer is a graduate of Edgewood College in Madison, Wisconsin. She attended Loyola University at Chicago and the University of California at Los Angeles. She holds elementary teaching certificates from the states of California and Oregon and has a life certificate from the state of California in parent education. She has worked as a Parent Educator for Los Angeles City Schools; served as Parent Educator on the Los Angeles Executive Board of Confraternity of Christian Doctrine and directed parenting programs for the Archdiocese of Los Angeles. At the present time she is teaching parenting classes for the Jackson County Mental Health Clinic in Medford, Oregon. She is the Parent Educator for Children's Services Division in the State of Oregon, training Parent Educators and teaching parenting classes for the agency. She also teaches workshops for churches, schools, community groups and agencies in Oregon and California.

I am deeply grateful to all the parents I have worked with, for I have learned much from them. Appreciation goes to my colleagues, who have reinforced my work. Heartfelt thanks goes to Lou Larsen, who took the time to type my work. Lastly, but most importantly, my loving gratitude goes to my husband and three children who have made parenting a joyful experience for me.